THE
POINT-TO-POINT
RECRUITS 2020/21

Jodie Standing

Published by
Marten Julian
69 Highgate, Kendal,
Cumbria, LA9 4ED
01539 741 007

rebecca@martenjulian.com
www.martenjulian.com

MARTEN JULIAN

1970 • 2020

Marten Julian (Publisher)
69 Highgate, Kendal, Cumbria LA9 4ED
www.martenjulian.com

First published in Great Britain in 2020

Copyright © Jodie Standing

A CIP catalogue record of this book is available from the British Library.

ISBN 978-1-8382317-0-5

ISSN 2633-2418 (Print)

Book Design & layout
Steve Dixon

Cover Photo Credit
JTW Equine Images

Firstly, let me start by thanking you for purchasing this third edition of *The Point-To-Point Recruits*. Your support is greatly appreciated and I hope that you find this book a useful source of reference for the coming season and beyond.

If I am honest, I can't quite believe this is the third year of writing the publication. I was researching for my 25 point-to-pointers to follow for *Marten Julian's Dark Horses Jumps Guide* when I first had the idea of expanding the list and putting them all in one place. Such was the quality of horses on offer I was finding it hard to whittle the numbers down, and consequently *The Point-To-Point Recruits* was born.

Unlike with horses who have raced under Rules, the point-to-point footage is not the most accessible and many of you will be seeing these names for the first time. With this book, I am trying to fill that void in the hope that it may give us a slight edge and earn us some profit along the way.

Despite the early curtailment of the season and with only a handful of four-year-old maidens run, I am pleasantly surprised at the quality of horses that I have managed to unearth. In this book I have expressed my opinion on 82 lightly raced individuals from the British and Irish pointing fields and amongst those are a special 20 which, in my view, have 'star potential'. This does not necessarily mean I believe they will all reach the highest level, but I expect them to do especially well for their new connections.

This year I have added two new features to the book. The first is 'The Look Back' which does exactly what it says on the tin – it looks back at the horses which featured in last year's publication. The second new feature is the 'The Course Glossary'. This section highlights all the courses which the horses featured have run at – whether they are undulating, flat, galloping, sharp…etc. Hopefully, it will prove an interesting but also useful tool when evaluating a horse's chance in a race under Rules.

As always, the writing of this book has been extremely enjoyable while also, at times, being somewhat absorbing. I would like to take this opportunity to thank Marten Julian for being a big support to me. I am also indebted to Rebecca Julian-Dixon, Steve Dixon, Ian Greensill, Alessandro Claus and everyone who took time to answer my queries at various stages along the way.

I also must say a special thank you to the photographers who have provided such wonderful images for this publication.

Finally, it just leaves me to say that I hope everyone has a successful, enjoyable and, most importantly, safe National Hunt season.

Best wishes

Jodie Standing

The following horses have all shown sufficient ability or potential to suggest they can make an impact under Rules for their new connections. As is the case with any horse, they will thrive at different stages of their careers. It may take time before some of them fulfil their potential while others may be precocious enough to win bumpers and novice hurdles this season.

A DISTANT PLACE
5YO BAY GELDING

TRAINER:	Jonjo O'Neill
PEDIGREE:	Sunday Break – South Africa (Turtle Bowl)
FORM:	3F1 -
OPTIMUM TRIP:	2m +
GOING:	Soft

A Distant Place will make his racecourse debut in the colours of J P McManus.

The John Staunton-trained gelding gained a deserved success at the third time of asking when returning the six-length winner of a five-year-old geldings' maiden at Carrigarostig in January having showed sufficient promise on his first two starts.

The bay – owned by Derek O'Connor's wife, Carol O'Donnell – suffered significant interference at the first fence on his debut at Dromahane which more or less took him out of the race. Derek then hunted him around at the back of the field before staying on eye-catchingly in the latter stages to finish a never-nearer third. A month later at Boulta, he looked set to improve on that performance but came down at the third from home when poised to make a bold challenge.

Finally off the mark in January, Derek O'Connor settled the five-year-old at the rear of the field, where he travelled within his comfort zone before edging closer to the pace on the long run from two out. Powering past the leaders on the outer before the final fence and appearing to have the race in safekeeping when his nearest pursuer fell, he came clear up the run-in to beat Mister Sweets by six lengths.

Out of a winning half-sister to French Grade 1 jumps winner, Top Of The Sky.

This £78,000 Goffs Doncaster Sales purchase doesn't look the biggest, but he's a hardy sort who possesses plenty of natural pace and also has abundant stamina.

A TIME TO SHINE
5YO BAY/BROWN GELDING

TRAINER:	Oliver Sherwood
PEDIGREE:	Malinas – Royal Bride (Kayf Tara)
FORM:	3 -
OPTIMUM TRIP:	2m +
GOING:	Soft

☆ **STAR POTENTIAL** ☆

A Time To Shine hails from a family full of winners and looks a good purchase for £70,000.

The athletically built son of Malinas created a favourable impression when embarking on his debut in a hotly contested four-year-olds' maiden at Knockmullen House in November 2019.

Trained by Sean Doyle and ridden by the five-pound claimer, Jamie Scallan, the gelding travelled comfortably in the mid-division for the main part of the race and was still held on to when producing a good leap over the fourth from home. Although niggled along to hold his position on the run to the next, he was back on the bridle by the time he reached the fence and once again came up well before progressing on to the heels of the leaders on the uphill part of the track.

Despite taking a little time to find top gear as the pace increased around the tight bend for home, he stuck to the task well and jumped the penultimate fence boldly before battling bravely on the run to the last. One final efficient leap helped to propel him up the run-in, where despite being no match for the winner, he was able to secure third place.

The race clocked a good time and the form has worked out well. The fourth, Do The Floss, and the eighth, One True King, both went on to win between the flags whilst the latter has also been successful under Rules at the first time of asking for Nigel Twiston-Davies and later finished tenth in the Champion Bumper at the Cheltenham Festival.

Out of an unraced sister to The Package, A Time To Shine is a full brother to Picanha – a bumper winner from last year's publication. That gelding needed plenty of time to strengthen and develop into his frame and it could be a similar story with A Time To Shine, who is not dissimilar in stature.

An exciting individual with the potential to develop into a lovely chaser down the line.

ACROSS THE CHANNEL
5YO BAY GELDING

TRAINER:	Philip Hobbs
PEDIGREE:	Dunkerque – Aulne River (River Mist)
FORM (P2P):	F1 -
OPTIMUM TRIP:	2m +
GOING:	Good To Soft

★ **STAR POTENTIAL** ★

Philip Hobbs has enjoyed plenty of success with this family.

Across The Channel looked booked for second place at best when falling at the final fence on his debut at Lisronagh in early November 2019 but atoned for that error when getting off the mark at Mainstown four weeks later.

Given a well-judged ride by Barry O'Neill, the gelding was never too far from the pace and jumped confidently before being asked to quicken on the long run to the second from home. Responding generously and taking aim at the more experienced long-time leader, the five-year-old landed within a length following a good leap and continued to accelerate alongside Junior Rattler. Gaining the upper hand approaching the last, Across The Channel met the fence on a good stride and battled valiantly all the way to the line to win by a neck with a three-length break back to the third, Upandatit.

There was quite a bit of depth to this race, with the runner-up – a second-season maiden – coming into the race having placed in a strong contest at Tinahely the time before. The third also had solid form having finished third to Fiston Des Issards on his debut.

Across The Channel is a half-brother to five winners, including Wait For Me and That's A Given, both of whom were trained by Philip Hobbs. Given his success with the family, it is of little surprise to see the Somerset-based trainer dig deep into his pockets and part with £150,000 at the Cheltenham Sale in December to take this gelding home.

There's a lot to like about Across The Channel, including his honest attitude. He also appears to have natural athleticism and plenty of scope. Interestingly his sire was a useful sprinter in France, which bodes well for a decent bumper campaign before switching to hurdles.

AHEAD OF THE FIELD
5YO CHESTNUT GELDING

TRAINER:	TBC
PEDIGREE:	Flemensfirth – Last Of The Bunch (Silver Patriarch)
FORM (P2P):	2 -
OPTIMUM TRIP:	2m 4f +
GOING:	Soft

A full brother to Champion Bumper winner, Relegate.

Ahead Of The Field showed plenty of potential when filling the runner-up spot behind the more experienced Es Perfecto on his debut at Tattersalls Farm in December 2019. Ridden prominently by Rob James, the Flemensfirth gelding produced a bold round of jumping in the testing conditions and still moved strongly when challenged for the lead by the eventual winner approaching the third from home.

Rallying gamely, the pair quickly opened up a considerable gap to the remainder and jumped the penultimate fence in unison before Ahead Of The Field's stamina wavered on the run to the last. He was eventually left to trail home 12 lengths behind the winner but 25 lengths ahead of the third.

For such an imposing individual this was a noteworthy debut performance and the winner has since highlighted the form by showing up well in a competitive bumper at Kempton for Alan King. The third, Wigglesworth, also went on to be second on his Rules debut.

As well as being a full brother to Relegate, Ahead Of The Field is a half-brother to Nicky Richards' promising young hurdler, Glenduff. His dam is a bumper/2m3f and 2m5f hurdle winner out of a bumper/2m hurdle winning sister to Better Times Ahead.

Led out of the sales ring unsold for £115,000 at Cheltenham in December 2019, it remains to be seen where he'll end up but he's a promising young horse with plenty to offer under Rules.

AMARILLO SKY
4YO BAY GELDING

TRAINER:	Colin Tizzard
PEDIGREE:	Westerner – Bag Of Tricks (Flemensfirth)
FORM (P2P):	1 -
OPTIMUM TRIP:	2m +
GOING:	Good to Soft

Amarillo Sky is the first of many young recruits to have joined Colin Tizzard.

The attractive white-faced son of Westerner produced a foot-perfect round of jumping on his debut in the first division of a competitive four-year-olds' maiden at Borris House in March where he came home the comfortable three-quarter-length winner from Tag Man with a further 15-length break back to the third, Hillview.

Colin Bowe's charge raced enthusiastically throughout the contest but got into a lovely rhythm over his fences before moving to the front on the final circuit. Continuing to bound along with ears pricked after taking the third from home, he then quickened on the bridle between the final two fences and readily held the runner-up under hands and heels riding from Barry O'Neill on the run to the line.

Amarillo Sky is the first foal out of Bag Of Tricks, a full sister to Beg To Differ who won over a range of trips up to three miles over hurdles and later developed into a very useful chaser over the same distances.

Purchased for £280,000 by Peter and Ross Doyle on behalf of Colin Tizzard.

He looks like he'll prove most effective over two miles on decent ground in his early career before developing into a chaser over a longer trip in time.

Amarillo Sky is the first foal out of Bag Of Tricks – a full sister to Beg To Differ. He could prove a useful sort for Colin Tizzard (Picture by Emma O'Brien)

BAREBACK JACK
4YO BAY GELDING

TRAINER:	Donald McCain
PEDIGREE:	Getaway – Dubh Go Leir (Definite Article)
FORM (P2P):	1 -
OPTIMUM TRIP:	2m
GOING:	Good to Soft

Bareback Jack started his career at Punchestown in February in a four-year-olds' maiden over 2m 4f where he was ridden patiently by Rob James and overcame a few ponderous leaps to win by an easy 15 lengths.

Forfeiting ground over the third from home and two out, the good-looking gelding showed superior speed between the fences and moved up to challenge around the turn for home where he and the leader pulled clear of the chasers. Flashing his tail in reply to a few cracks of the whip, the four-year-old accelerated on the approach to the last and seemingly had the race in safekeeping when his nearest pursuer fell, leaving him to come clear up the run-in where he continued to flash his tail.

Despite not being the most fluent over his fences, Bareback Jack clearly had too much pace for his opposition and always looked the likely winner turning for home. His tail flashing could suggest a slight quirk or lack of maturity.

Out of the bumper/2m hurdle winner, Dubh Go Leir, herself a sister to bumper/2m4f-3m hurdle winner Dubh Eile. The further family link back to the high-class hurdler Mighty Mogul.

Purchased for €40,000 as a three-year-old, he has since been sold to Donald McCain for £70,000 and will now carry the colours of Tim Leslie.

Bareback Jack looks a classy recruit and providing he can continue to develop mentally, he should have more than enough speed to land a bumper or two this season.

BOLD CONDUCT
5YR BAY GELDING

TRAINER:	Colin Tizzard
PEDIGREE:	Stowaway – Vics Miller (Old Vic)
FORM (P2P):	1 -
OPTIMUM TRIP:	2m 4f +
GOING:	Soft

Bold Conduct featured in last year's publication but never made it to the track.

The son of Stowaway towered above his opposition as he made his debut in an above-average four-year-olds' maiden at Loughanmore in November 2018 where the pace was ferocious from the outset.

Richie Deegan ensured his mount settled into a good rhythm in the early stages and bided his time in the middle of the pack before progressing through the field as the race developed. Still hard on the steel at five out, the gelding glided into third place at the fourth from home and continued to hold that position before lengthening his stride to take him into second as he produced a decent leap at the penultimate fence.

The tempo increased significantly on the long swing into the home straight as Sidi Ismael attempted to put the race to bed, but Bold Conduct's ground-eating stride enabled him to keep tabs on the leader before jumping to the front over the last and stretching clear up the run-in to win by two and a half lengths with a further 12 back to the third.

This was a properly run race which clocked the fastest time set on the day by some margin. The form also looks strong as the second, third and fourth have all been successful since.

A full brother to Harry Whittington's Speedy Cargo who has placed twice from five starts under Rules. His dam is an unraced half-sister to 2m1f-3m6f hurdle/ chase (including cross-country) winner Maljimar, bumper/2m-3m hurdle/ useful chaser winner Kymandjen and bumper/useful 2m3f-2m5f hurdle/chase winner Like A Lion.

I had a good look at Bold Conduct as he paraded around the sales ring at Cheltenham where he sold to Colin Tizzard for £150,000. He really is a humongous individual, not gangly or ungainly but a powerhouse who will undoubtedly take time to fill his frame. It's a testament to his natural ability that he was able to show so much, never mind win a point-to-point at such an early stage of his development.

I presume the reason we have not seen him is because he has been given plenty of time to develop. He remains an exciting prospect with the potential to go far.

BRANDY LOVE
4YO BAY FILLY

TRAINER:	Willie Mullins
PEDIGREE:	Jet Away – Bambootcha (Saddlers' Hall)
FORM (P2P):	1 -
OPTIMUM TRIP:	2m +
GOING:	Soft

Brandy Love returned an impressive winner on her debut in the colours of Colin Bowe's Milestone Partnership.

The four-year-old by Jet Away – a three-part brother to Dansili – took on the geldings in a 2m 4f maiden at Cragmore in February. Always travelling in her comfort zone, the filly displayed plenty of natural agility over her fences and superior speed to gradually pull away from the field on the uphill run to two from home. Despite getting in a little tight, her momentum remained intact and she continued to extend on the bridle to the final fence, which she popped over nicely before crossing the line eight lengths to the good over Just A Dime.

Although not the biggest and unlikely to develop into a scopey chaser, Brandy Love is a well-made type with plenty of athleticism and should have no problem when dropping back in trip under Rules. She also appears to have inherited the willing and unrelenting attitude of her sire which will stand her in good stead in the heat of a battle.

Brandy Love proved popular at the Cheltenham Sale in February when selling the way of Willie Mullins' bloodstock agent, Harold Kirk, who saw off Tom Malone to secure the filly for a hefty £200,000.

From a winning family, she is a half-sister to the three-time winner, Topofthecotswolds, trained by Nigel Twiston-Davies, the Noel Meade-trained Getaway Kid and the David Kelly-trained Anna Holty.

I am sure Willie Mullins will find plenty of winning opportunities for Brandy Love. I imagine they'll start her off in a bumper.

Brandy Love parading ahead of being sold at Cheltenham in February (Picture by Tattersalls)

BRAVE WAY
5YO BAY MARE

TRAINER:	Henry De Bromhead
PEDIGREE:	Jeremy – Black Mariah (Bob's Return)
FORM (P2P):	1 -
OPTIMUM TRIP:	2m 2f +
GOING:	Good to Soft

An unbeaten mare set to carry the colours of Cheltenham Festival-winning owner Kenneth Alexander.

The Warren Ewing-trained Brave Way was one of six newcomers when making her winning debut in a 10-runner four-year-old mares' maiden at Knockinroe at the end of October 2019.

Always towards the fore, the daughter of the late Jeremy displayed good tactical speed upon touching down over the fourth from home and burrowed her way through a gap to move into second position. From there she continued to track the leader, and although losing a length after making an untidy shape at the next, she quickly regained momentum on the level and nipped up the inside on the turn out of the back straight.

An efficient leap over the penultimate fence took her to the lead before being challenged by the well-supported favourite on the approach to the last. Belying her greenness, Brave Way stuck to her task gamely to fend off Uptown Lady and produced a better leap over the final fence to maintain her length advantage all the way to the line.

Purchased for €10,000 at the Doncaster Spring Sale as a three-year-old store, Warren Ewing received a hefty return for his money when she went under the hammer to Rathmore Stud for £160,000 in November 2019 at Cheltenham's Sale.

A half-sister to a point winner and 2m-2m5f Listed hurdle winner Coillte Lass. Her dam is a half-sister to the Martin Pipe-trained multi-Graded winner, Classified.

Brave Way's belated Rules debut may be due to the relentless wet winter. No doubt still in the process of developing physically, the time away will have done her world of good and I expect her to make a good start to her career over hurdles.

BROOKSWAY FAIR
4YO BAY GELDING

TRAINER:	Evan Williams
PEDIGREE:	Mahler – Brook Style (Alderbrook)
FORM (P2P):	2 -
OPTIMUM TRIP:	2m 4f +
GOING:	Soft

A full brother to Warren Greatrex's useful hurdler, Mahlervous.

Brooksway Fair looked a strong stayer when getting up in the closing stages to make a winning debut in a 2m 4f maiden at Knockmullen House in early February.

Ridden patiently in the testing conditions by Jamie Codd, the gelding made steady progress on the final circuit and jumped into fifth position over the fourth from home before advancing into second place with a quick leap over the next. Soon on the heels of the long-time leader on the steep climb towards the home straight, the bay needed rousing along to find top gear but jumped the penultimate fence well and battled bravely on the run to the last, pulling out a little extra and gaining the upper hand on the approach. A courageous leap ensured he maintained his momentum which carried him to the line for a hard-fought two-length success over Orbys Legend.

Brooksway Fair needed every yard of this trip and looks a big, raw horse who will ultimately develop into a strong stayer.

Evan Williams paid £80,000 to take him home from the Cheltenham Sale in February and I can see him acting around tracks such as Ffos Las and Chepstow.

He's one for the future.

CARRIG COPPER
6YO BAY GELDING

TRAINER:	TBC
PEDIGREE:	Presenting – Copper Dusht (Dushyantor)
FORM (P2P):	2 -
OPTIMUM TRIP:	2m +
GOING:	Good to Soft

An older gelding who could slip under the radar.

Carrig Copper was well supported when making his debut for Terence O'Brien in a 10-runner five-year-olds' maiden at Dromahane in November 2019 but was just touched off in a sprint to the line.

The son of Presenting travelled notably well for the duration of the race and moved up to take closer order after jumping the fourth from home. Still hard on the bridle, the bay produced fantastic leaps over the next two fences but was caught a little flat-footed as the leader quickened down to the last. Despite taking a stride or two to find top gear, he moved up to the eventual winner's quarters on the take-off and battled gamely on the run to the line but couldn't find the extra gear needed to go by and was defeated by a neck.

The winner, Eklat De Rire, went on to finish second in a maiden hurdle on his debut for Henry De Bromhead before getting off the mark in fine style when upped in trip to 2m 7f. The third, One More Life, was placed on his next two pointing starts, whilst the sixth (beaten 27 lengths), went on to win a maiden in January.

Carrig Copper comes from a lovely family and is a half-brother to the sadly ill-fated Copper Gone West. His dam is a half-sister to the useful Presenting Copper and Copper Bleu.

Being a son of Presenting, Carrig Copper will probably be more at home on better ground than he experienced in his point.

He looks a natural chaser and a lovely horse to follow.

CHOSEN PORT
4YO BAY FILLY

TRAINER:	Olly Murphy
PEDIGREE:	Well Chosen – Despute (Be My Native)
FORM (P2P):	1 -
OPTIMUM TRIP:	2m +
GOING:	Soft

Chosen Port accounted for a competitive eight-runner four-year-old mares' maiden five days prior to being sold at the Cheltenham Festival Sale for £115,000.

The daughter of Well Chosen is a petite filly but is athletically built and coped well with the softening ground conditions under Barry O'Neill at Ballycahane in March. Clearly knowing her job, she jumped professionally and moved strongly throughout the contest before taking closer order after the third from home. Delaying her move to challenge for the lead until the run to the final fence, she quickened smartly and reeled in the long-time pacesetter, Western Zara, before popping over the fence nicely and kept on well to the line to win by two lengths.

Following her victory, Colin Bowe said, "This is a mare we've liked since the day we got her. She's very professional altogether. We think she's very smart."

A full sister to Venetia Williams' Burtons Well and bumper winner Ratheniska. She is also closely related to Blazing Port and is a half-sister to the high-class Burton Port.

Given her useful turn of foot, Chosen Port could produce some smart form in bumpers, especially against her own gender before stepping up in trip over hurdles and later fences.

The well-related Chosen Port leaping her way to victory at Ballycahane (Picture by Leah O'Carroll)

CLONDAW BERTIE
5YO BAY GELDING

TRAINER:	Mouse Morris
PEDIGREE:	Thewayyouare – Female (Saddlers' Hall)
FORM:	1 - 5
OPTIMUM TRIP:	2m +
GOING:	Soft

A flashy gelding with a bright future.

The white-faced son of Thewayyouare created a lasting impression when coming home a wide margin winner of the four-year-old geldings' maiden at Dromahane in late December, recording a time five seconds faster than the second division.

Shane Fitzgerald rode the gelding off the pace for much of the contest before making an eye-catching move after jumping the fourth from home. Surging through the field to pick up the running in the blink of an eye, the sudden injection of pace caught those in behind on the hop and suddenly Clondaw Bertie was a few lengths clear of the chasing group as he popped over the third last.

Continuing to pull away on the short run to the next, an untidy leap did little to interrupt his progress and he bounded down to the last. At that point he had the race in safekeeping when his nearest pursuer fell, leaving him to coast home 12 lengths to the good over Get Your Own.

The gelding has since made his Rules debut in a Punchestown maiden hurdle where he shaped with plenty of encouragement and moved through to lead on the bridle at the penultimate flight before weakening on the run to the last.

Mouse Morris does not rush his horses and will have left plenty to work on with Clondaw Bertie, which makes his first appearance in the colours of Robcour all the more pleasing.

Clondaw Bertie hails from a family full of winners. His half-brothers include 2m2f-2m4f hurdle/chase winner Coolaghknock Glebe, 2m1f hurdle/chase winner Act In Time, and 2m-2m5f hurdle/chase winner Neddyvaughan. His dam was a bumper and hurdle winner over two miles and is a half-sister to the high-class 2m-2m4f chaser Direct Route.

I fully expect Clondaw Bertie to improve for his first outing on the racecourse and believe he has the potential to develop into a very decent performer in the future.

CLONDAW SECRET
5YO BAY GELDING

TRAINER:	Gordon Elliott
PEDIGREE:	Court Cave – Secret Can't Say (Jurado)
FORM (P2P):	1 -
OPTIMUM TRIP:	2m +
GOING:	Good to Soft

Gordon Elliott has several talented looking individuals to go to war with this season, and Clondaw Secret is right up there.

Michael Goff's gelding was well backed to make a winning debut at Boulta in December and he didn't disappoint his supporters when staying on stoutly at the end of the three miles to win by two lengths.

The five-year-old by Court Cave raced towards the rear in the early stages under Shane Fitzgerald and made steady progress into eighth place passing the halfway point. Moving fluently as he progressed through the field, he quickly assumed a share of third position on the long run to the cross fence, three from home, where a good leap advanced his position further.

Ridden along entering the straight but responding willingly, the gelding took up the running with a good leap over the penultimate fence but was made to battle by the long-time leader on the run to the last. Showing resilience and pulling out extra, he produced a good jump over the fence and asserted up the run-in to beat the more experienced Champagne Gold with something in hand, recording a time five seconds quicker than the second division.

Clondaw Secret benefited from a well-judged ride on ground officially described as soft/heavy. The patient tactics certainly helped conserve the horse's energy and enabled him to pick off the leader who had always been towards the fore. The form also received a boost when the fourth won next time by six lengths.

With a total of six full brothers the breeder obviously likes to cross the mare with Court Cave. The best of those siblings is Clondaw Court, a four-time winner for Willie Mullins (bumper/2m2f-2m6f hurdle). Other winners include Peacocks Secret (bumper/2m2f-2m4f jumps) and Just Cause (2m4f/2m6f hurdle).

Clondaw Secret has a nice way of going. He also looks to possess a sizable frame and will ultimately develop into a chaser much further down the line. In the meantime, judging by his pedigree, I would expect him to be competitive in a bumper or novices' hurdle over trips up to 2m 4f.

A special moment between Clondaw Secret and his handler prior to being sold (Photo by Tattersalls)

COOTHILL
5YO BAY GELDING

TRAINER:	TBC
PEDIGREE:	Yeats – Moll Bawn (Presenting)
FORM (P2P):	3 -
OPTIMUM TRIP:	2m +
GOING:	Good to Soft

Coothill shaped with eye-catching promise on his only start and looks a likely improver.

The Yeats gelding made his debut for Colin McKeever in the colours of Wilson Dennison in a four-year-olds' maiden at Turtulla where he finished third, six lengths behind Scene Not Herd who has since posted a solid performance under Rules in a bumper for Charlie Longsdon.

Held up off the pace for most of the race, the bay was ridden to improve after the fourth from home and jumped three out in fifth place. Advancing into third before the penultimate fence, he put distance between himself and the fourth on the run to the last and closed on the second all the way up the run-in, crossing the line in the manner of a horse with more to give.

This looked a good race and the form has held up well with the fourth, Champagne Gold, finishing a good second in a strong maiden next time, whilst the sixth, Minella Lightning, went on to win a maiden by 30 lengths.

Closely related to 2m7f chase winner Glenwood Prince and bumper/2m hurdle winner Royal Moll. He is also a half-brother to bumper winner, Ballygomartin. His dam is an unraced half-sister to smart bumper/2m-3m1f hurdle/chase winner Calling Brave and smart staying chaser, Ottowa.

Coothill's pedigree suggests he'll show up well in a bumper but given his time away from the track, his new connections will probably be keen to press on over hurdles. He looks to have plenty of potential.

CORRAN CROSS
5YO BAY GELDING

TRAINER:	Gordon Elliott
PEDIGREE:	Doyen – Steel Lady (Gamut)
FORM (P2P):	1 -
OPTIMUM TRIP:	2m +
GOING:	Soft

Corran Cross provided Jamie Codd with the first leg of his treble when winning the opening four-year-olds' maiden at Tinahely in November.

The pace was strong from the outset but the attractive son of Doyen always travelled smoothly behind the leaders and jumped confidently. After doing well to avoid a faller at the third from home, he took closer order on the long run to the next and showed smart speed to close on the leader's quarters before brushing through the top of the fence. Despite the mistake, he knuckled down well on the landing side and renewed his challenge on the short run to the last, gaining the upper hand going into the wings of the fence before popping over nicely and sticking to his task determinedly on the run-in to win by two lengths.

There was plenty to like about this performance. Not only did Corran Cross look professional in the way he travelled and jumped, he also displayed a potent turn of foot and the courage to battle in the latter stages. The race – which clocked a good time – also worked out well with the third and seventh both going on to win, whilst the runner-up was narrowly beaten in a strong maiden next time.

The Doyen gelding is the first foal out of a half-sister to the sadly ill-fated smart 2m-2m3f hurdle/chase winner Real Steel, 1m6f Flat/useful 2m-2m4f hurdle winner Grangeclare Gold and useful 2m3f/2m4f hurdle winner Up For The Match.

Bought for €13,000 from the Land Rover Sale as a three-year-old, he has since passed through the ring at Cheltenham in December 2019 for £130,000 selling the way of Aidan O'Ryan standing alongside Gordon Elliott.

This looks a classy sort and I have high hopes for him reaching a decent level, especially on soft ground.

DEPLOY THE GETAWAY
5YO BAY GELDING

TRAINER:	Willie Mullins
PEDIGREE:	Getaway – Gaelic River (Deploy)
FORM (P2P):	1 -
OPTIMUM TRIP:	2m +
GOING:	Soft

This gelding featured in last year's publication but never made it to the track after meeting with a setback. Thankfully, he is now back in training and he should have no problem making up for lost time.

The physically imposing son of Getaway started his career in a four-year-olds' maiden at Tallow in February 2019 for Donnchadh Doyle and James Walsh where he was simply in a different stratosphere to his opposition. Booted to the front as the flags went up, the bay was relentless on the front end, jumping with foot-perfect precision and gaining ground at each fence. He still only appeared to be travelling in second gear as he jumped four out with ears pricked and a five-length lead quickly doubled after he sailed over the third from home. By the time he had reached the next, the race was in safekeeping and a mistake at the last did very little to interrupt his momentum as he coasted home to a heavily eased 20-length success.

This really was a head-turning performance and there was no surprise to see him fetch plenty of interest at the Cheltenham Sale in February. Tom Malone and Tessa Greatrex all wanted a piece of the action, but it was Harold Kirk who had the final say when signing the docket to a sum of £200,000. The gelding will now run in the colours of Cheveley Park Stud for trainer Willie Mullins.

The gelding has an impressive pedigree to match his performance. His dam is an unraced half-sister to 3m/3m6f chase winner Bally Braes out of an unraced half-sister to bumper/2m6f-3m3f hurdle/chase winner Special Account and useful 2m4f-3m1f chase winner River Mandalay. From the family of Special Tiara.

Deploy The Getaway obviously has a huge engine and a high cruising speed. His round knee action may lend itself to soft underfoot conditions, but this is a high-class individual and I expect him to be making his way through the ranks to Graded company over the coming seasons.

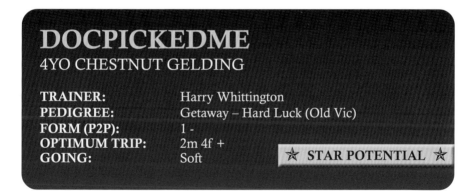

DOCPICKEDME
4YO CHESTNUT GELDING

TRAINER:	Harry Whittington
PEDIGREE:	Getaway – Hard Luck (Old Vic)
FORM (P2P):	1 -
OPTIMUM TRIP:	2m 4f +
GOING:	Soft

★ **STAR POTENTIAL** ★

A really likeable individual who won with something in hand on debut.

Docpickedme made his pointing debut in a four-year-old geldings' maiden at Ballycahane in early March where he was ridden by Derek O'Connor in the colours of Paul Holden for Ellmarie Holden.

Having started in a prominent position, the pair gradually lost their pitch and were shuffled back through the field into sixth place at the halfway point. On and off the bridle at various stages but jumping well, the gelding edged closer to the pace on the run to the penultimate fence where he was aided by a slick leap which propelled him around the turn for home.

Using his lengthy stride and motivated by his rider, the four-year-old found top gear once straightened up and gathered in the leaders on the run to the last.

A bold leap there helped him land with plenty of momentum which he carried up the run-in to record a very game one-length success from Patroclus who went on to fetch £150,000 at the Cheltenham Festival Sale in March.

Docpickedme was sold at the same sale for what looks a good price at £75,000, going the way of J D Moore on behalf of Harry Whittington.

This gelding is a half-brother to Kim Bailey's strong stayer, Another Venture, out of an unraced half-sister to 3m-3m1f chase winner Monty's Quest and 2m3f hurdle winner Timmy Allen.

Although his distant family all have winning form on good ground, Docpickedme's round knee action may lend itself better to ground with plenty of give. I expect the four-year-old to show plenty of promise this season, but we will not see the best of him until he tackles fences later in his career. He's a nice individual to look forward to.

ELMDALE
6YO GREY GELDING

TRAINER:	Nigel Twiston-Davies
PEDIGREE:	Martaline – Victoire Jaguine (Saint Des Saints)
FORM (P2P):	3/2F2 -
OPTIMUM TRIP:	3m
GOING:	Soft

A real giant of a horse.

Elmdale is not an obvious inclusion in this publication and judging by the size of him, it could be some time before we see his true potential.

Despite remaining a maiden after four starts between the flags, the grey has showed a good amount of potential. Firstly, he finished third on his debut at Kirkistown in February 2019 to Gold Des Bois who has since placed three times over hurdles for Jessica Harrington. He then chased home the promising Do Your Job on his seasonal reappearance at Castletown-Geoghegan where he jumped well but lacked the pace of the winner in the latter stages. A faller next time when well supported in the market at Loughanmore, he then rounded off his pointing career with another creditable placed effort, this time at Lisronagh where he chased home Crossing Lines, who has won again by 20 lengths and now enters training with David Pipe.

On each occasion Elmdale travelled well throughout his races and although he lacked the tactical pace to win, he stayed on gamely to reach the frame and highlighted himself as a potential improver when encountering suitable conditions under Rules.

Now in the care of Nigel Twiston-Davies who excels with this sort of horse, I envisage he will start his career over hurdles where he'll earn a handicap rating before perhaps switching to novice handicap chases.

He's a slow burner, but I have high hopes for him being a great success for his new connections.

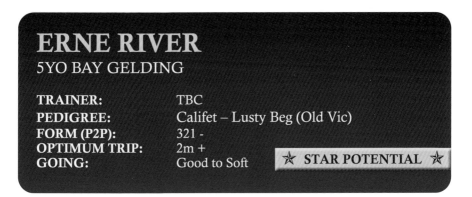

ERNE RIVER
5YO BAY GELDING

TRAINER:	TBC
PEDIGREE:	Califet – Lusty Beg (Old Vic)
FORM (P2P):	321 -
OPTIMUM TRIP:	2m +
GOING:	Good to Soft

☆ **STAR POTENTIAL** ☆

Erne River progressed with each of his three runs and could slip under the radar.

Colin Bowe's charge showed a decent level of ability when staying on from off the pace to grab third place behind Corran Cross on his debut at Tinahely in November, and improved upon that effort two weeks later to finish second at Mainstown where he was collared two from home by the very useful-looking Hes A Hardy Bloke.

Putting his experience to good use, the Califet gelding finally got off the mark when allowed to dictate a five-runner maiden at Dungarvan in January. Booted to the front from the drop of the flag, the bay jumped cleanly and showed plenty of pace to quicken after a slick leap over the third from home. With something up his sleeve, he was able to fend off a challenger on the run to the penultimate fence and stretched clear again over the last before crossing the line with more in hand that the one-and-a-half-length winning margin suggests.

Erne River showed a really likeable attitude and a good blend of speed and stamina to get the job done. It wasn't the strongest contest but it's a long way home from the back of the last and I like the way he kept pulling out extra.

The five-year-old is a half-brother to Passageway, a son of Stowaway who made a winning track debut in a bumper at the 2018 Punchestown Festival for Willie Mullins where he beat subsequent Grade 1 Cheltenham Festival winners City Island and Minella Indo. His dam is a half-sister to Munster National winner Treacle, Green Belt Flyer and Lucky Bay, all of whom were successful up to three miles.

I like this individual very much and I would expect him to show up well in a bumper. Equally, if connections chose to send him straight over hurdles his experience will not be lost on him. He may be best suited to better ground.

FABRIQUE EN FRANCE
5YO BAY GELDING

TRAINER:	Olly Murphy
PEDIGREE:	Yeats – Knar Mardy (Erhaab)
FORM (P2P):	372 -
OPTIMUM TRIP:	2m
GOING:	Soft

Fabrique En France is an experienced sort who remains a maiden despite showing plenty of ability.

The five-year-old Yeats gelding finished third, beaten 12 and a half lengths, on his debut at Stowlin in May 2019 where he shaped eye-catchingly on the final circuit before weakening on the run to the last.

Put away for the summer, he reappeared under Jamie Codd at Ballindenisk in January where again he shaped encouragingly and made good progress over the third from home but was unable to sustain his effort on the heavy ground.

Benefiting from those experiences, he created a more favourable impression on his most recent start at Ballycahane when finishing with a late rattle to get within three lengths of the £300,000 Cheltenham Festival Sale topper, Killer Kane. Again ridden by Jamie Codd, he was anchored towards the rear for the majority of the contest before easing himself into the race after the third from home. Still with plenty to do jumping two out, he made rapid progress on fresh ground approaching the last but ran out of time to collar the leader on the short run to the line.

Fabrique En France could slip under the radar when he embarks on a career under Rules for Olly Murphy. He is not short of pace and will probably prove most effective over a shorter trip.

FASHION NOVA
5YO GREY MARE

TRAINER:	Fergal O'Brien
PEDIGREE:	Flemensfirth – Fashion's Worth (Great Palm)
FORM (P2P):	41 -
OPTIMUM TRIP:	2m 4f +
GOING:	Soft

 ☆ **STAR POTENTIAL** ☆

A gutsy mare with stamina to burn.

Fashion Nova shaped with plenty of promise on her debut at Borris House in December 2019, staying on from well off the pace to finish fourth having been caught a little unawares when the pace increased with two fences to take.

She then went to Bellharbour in February where she was partnered by Rob James who rode her with confidence up with the pace before moving through to lead after the sixth from home. The pair stole a couple of lengths on the field with a fluent leap over five out and continued to hold that advantage until getting in tight to the next. With momentum soon restored, she continued to bowl along in front, eating up the ground with her lengthy stride and extended her lead on the uphill climb to three out where another bold jump helped maintain her momentum before she produced a spring-heeled leap over the penultimate fence.

Gamely keeping up the gallop on the downhill part of the track, the mare was strongly pressed moving through the gap in the wall on the run to the last, but she battled bravely and came up with one final fluent leap which helped propel her up the run-in and force a dead-heat with Rose Milan.

There was so much to like about this sound-jumping grey mare's performance and Fergal O'Brien looks to have got a steal of a price when paying £48,000 for her at Cheltenham in February.

Out of a half-sister to Gold Cup winner Bobs Worth from the family of French 1,000 Guineas winner, Ukraine Girl.

I would expect Fashion Nova to be suited to a variety of trips. Her willing attitude is an asset to her

Fergal O'Brien casting his eye over a potential new purchase. He could have smart prospect on his hands with Fashion Nova (Picture by Tattersalls)

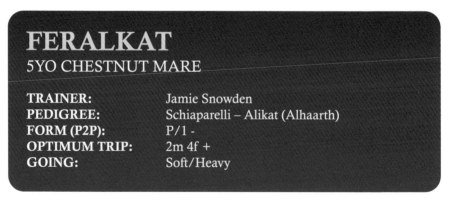

FERALKAT
5YO CHESTNUT MARE

TRAINER:	Jamie Snowden
PEDIGREE:	Schiaparelli – Alikat (Alhaarth)
FORM (P2P):	P/1 -
OPTIMUM TRIP:	2m 4f +
GOING:	Soft/Heavy

Feralkat is a solid stamp of a horse.

The daughter of Schiaparelli started her career in the care of David Kelly for whom she made her debut at Rathcannon in April 2019 but failed to make an impression and was pulled up with two fences to jump.

Switched to Denis Hogan's base in Tipperary, she reappeared in November at Moig South and improved plenty for her summer's break to win under the trainer's nephew, Jack Hogan.

Displaying a tremendously game attitude in the testing conditions, the mare took closer order after four out and was ridden along at various stages in second place before rounding the turn for home. Responding generously to press for the lead over the penultimate fence, she took a slender advantage upon touching down and battled determinedly approaching the last, jumping the fence in her stride before sticking on tenaciously to record a hard-fought one-and-a-half-length victory over Ballycallan Fame.

The form has been let down since, but this was a thoroughly commendable effort from the then four-year-old. She has a sizable frame to fill and undoubtedly needed the run on her debut. She will require further time to fully mature and with that improvement can be expected.

Sold for £90,000 at Cheltenham's November Sale, she is a half-sister to the Grade 1 Punchestown Champion Bumper winner, The Liquidator, who later went on to win over hurdles up to 2m1f. Her dam was a 2m3f-3m2f hurdle/chase winner and is a half-sister to an Italian 10.5f Listed winner.

Judging by her pedigree she clearly is not devoid of pace, but I see her as more of a stayer with a love for the deep midwinter mud. Her attitude will stand her in good stead.

FILE ILLICO
5YO BAY GELDING

TRAINER:	Jonjo O'Neill
PEDIGREE:	Cokoriko – Noryane (Dom Alco)
FORM (P2P):	1 -
OPTIMUM TRIP:	2m 4f +
GOING:	Good to Soft

This son of Cokoriko has the pedigree to develop into a staying chaser.

File Illico made light work of a six-runner field on his debut at Knockanard in February – a meeting which was halted after the third race due to the increasing strong winds.

The Michael Goff-trained newcomer tracked the leader for the most part of the race before sauntering up to challenge on the approach to the fourth from home where he produced a good leap to move alongside the Tom Keating-trained Three Nations. Still hard on the bridle as the pace increased on the downhill part of the track, the son of Cokoriko comprehensively outjumped his rival over the third from home and touched down a couple of lengths to the good.

From there his dominance only grew and a five-length lead at the penultimate fence quickly doubled as he powered up the steep hill before swinging into the straight and popping over the last. Shaken up on the landing side, the gelding extended impressively indicating he had plenty left in the tank as he crossed the line a distance clear of Salt Wind, who was the only other finisher.

The five-year-old missed last season after cutting himself but he is quickly making up for lost time and was snapped up by Jonjo O'Neill for a modest £58,000 at Cheltenham's February Sale.

A close relation to the strong stayer Mister Apple's, I would expect File Illico to need time to fully reach his potential, but I hope he shows up well over hurdles this season.

FISHKHOV
5YO CHESTNUT GELDING

TRAINER:	Harry Fry
PEDIGREE:	Sholokhov – Kavalle (Video Rock)
FORM (P2P):	2 -
OPTIMUM TRIP:	2m 4f +
GOING:	Soft

Fishkhov had to settle for the runner-up spot on his debut at Dromahane in December where he bumped into a talented-looking sort in Vanillier from the Sam Curling yard.

The strongly built chestnut was ridden patiently towards the rear under Derek O'Connor for the main part of the race but edged closer over the fourth from home before progressing further with a good leap over the next.

Asked for an effort on the run to the penultimate fence, the response was immediate with the gelding quickly latching himself on to the front runners before jumping into a share of the lead. Looking the likely winner approaching

the last, he again came up well but was outbattled on the run to the line by
the grey who showed plenty of resolve to claw back the advantage after being
headed.

This was a really pleasing debut from Fishkhov and the form received a couple
of boosts with the fourth and fifth both winning subsequently.

A half-brother to French 2m2f chase and 2m7f cross-country chase winner
Dimanche Morning. His dam is an 11.7f AQPS Flat/2m1f chase winner out
of an unraced half-sister to a 3m/3m1f chase winner.

Fishkhov's sizable frame and stout pedigree suggests he'll need a trip to be seen
at his best. That said, the change of gear he produced between the final two
fences will lend itself nicely to a bumper if connections choose to go down that
route. He also appears to possess a thoroughly likeable attitude.

FISTON DES ISSARDS
5YO BAY/BROWN GELDING

TRAINER:	Gordon Elliott
PEDIGREE:	Buck's Boum – Saboum (Robin Des Champs)
FORM (P2P):	1 -
OPTIMUM TRIP:	2m +
GOING:	Good to Soft

☆ **STAR POTENTIAL** ☆

A striking-looking gelding with the potential to make a big impact in the
colours of Robcour this season.

Fiston Des Issards created an impression which lives long in the memory
when winning on debut for Colin Bowe and jockey Barry O'Neill in a strong
10-runner four-year-old geldings' maiden at Loughanmore towards the end of
October 2019.

Sent off at odds of 6/1, the Buck's Boum gelding moved with purpose behind
the leaders before edging into a slender advantage going out on to the final
circuit. With ears pricked, he came up out of his jockey's hands over the fourth
from home and maintained his lead with another foot-perfect leap over the next
where the field attempted to close.

Running green at times but responding to pressure from the saddle, he asserted
his advantage around the home bend and pulled further clear under hands and

heels riding on the run to the last fence where a final perfect leap left the race in no doubt as he cleared away to win by a comfortable three and a half lengths.

Not only was this a visually impressive performance, the form has worked out exceptionally well. The runner-up, Boothill, went on to win a Kempton bumper by a little over four lengths on his Rules debut for Harry Fry, the third home went on to fill the same position in his next point whilst the fourth home, Smurphy Enki, thwarted his opposition in a Warwick bumper by 18 lengths on his debut for Chris Gordon.

Fiston Des Issards is a big horse for a first foal. He is also very athletic and lengthy with plenty of frame to fill. I'm sure connections will find a winning opportunity for him this season, whether it be in bumpers or over hurdles. I believe he has the potential to develop into a Festival horse.

FLAME BEARER
5YO BAY GELDING

TRAINER:	TBC
PEDIGREE:	Fame And Glory – Banba (Docksider)
FORM (P2P):	2 -
OPTIMUM TRIP:	2m
GOING:	Soft

Flame Bearer looks sure to improve on his eye-catching debut at Borris House in March.

Donnchadh Doyle's five-year-old was one of just two newcomers in the 10-strong line-up but displayed no signs of inexperience in his quest to make all and held a commanding 10-length lead at the third from home. Having jumped and travelled with confidence until that point, his stamina began to wane on the run to the penultimate fence and his lead was gradually eroded to three lengths by the time he left the ground.

Lacking nothing in courage as he battled bravely on the run to the last, he was unaided by an untidy leap over the fence which allowed his more experienced rival to overhaul him on the run-in and eventually win by a length.

This was a hugely commendable debut performance from Flame Bearer whose pedigree suggest three miles would stretch his stamina to the limit. From a family full of Flat performers, his half-brothers were successful over trips ranging from five furlongs right up to a mile and a quarter. His dam was also an 86-rated 1m/9.7f winner.

Purchased expensively for €78,000 at the prestigious Derby Sale in Ireland in June 2018, he has probably been sold privately throughout the summer and it remains to be seen where he will end up this term.

I fully expect he'll have enough speed to win a bumper, but connections may press on with him over hurdles. He could be useful.

FUEGO DE L'ABBAYE
5YO BAY GELDING

TRAINER:	TBC
PEDIGREE:	Kap Rock – Marsavrile (April Night)
FORM (P2P):	U1 -
OPTIMUM TRIP:	2m +
GOING:	Good to Soft

A graduate from Baltimore Stables who appears to possess a touch of class.

Fuego De L'Abbaye got off the mark in good style at the second time of asking at Dowth Hall in October 2019, having got no further than the second fence on his debut at Bartlemy in May earlier that year.

The four-year-old raced keenly in the very early stages but settled better once taken to the front by Luke Murphy and got into a good rhythm over his fences. Still cruising along with a two-length lead after jumping the fifth from home, the bay continued to hold his advantage over the next couple of fences before easing further ahead on the run to two out. Despite getting in a little tight, he had plenty left up his sleeve to regather his momentum on the uphill run to the last, which he popped over nicely with a length to spare over his nearest pursuer before pulling away again up the run-in to win by two lengths.

Out of a dam who was placed over 13.5f in a French AQPS Flat race. Her sister was the 11.5f-12.5f Flat/2m4f-3m1f winner Petit Bob out of a French 1m2f and 1m4f Flat/2m hurdle and 2m2f chase winner.

Fuego De L'Abbaye was led out of the Cheltenham Sales ring unsold for £48,000 in November.

Naturally athletic with a good deal of speed in his family, he will be seen to best effect over shorter distances.

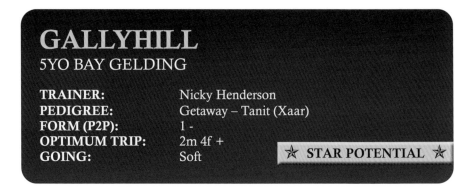

GALLYHILL
5YO BAY GELDING

TRAINER:	Nicky Henderson
PEDIGREE:	Getaway – Tanit (Xaar)
FORM (P2P):	1 -
OPTIMUM TRIP:	2m 4f +
GOING:	Soft

☆ **STAR POTENTIAL** ☆

Gallyhill will be in everyone's notebook this season.

The good-looking son of Getaway provided new handler Jamie Sloan – who took over the reins from Ian Ferguson at Loughanmore Farm in County Antrim – with the perfect start to his training career at Kirkistown in late November.

On paper it looked a strong division of the four-year-old geldings' maiden, with Colin Bowe, Stuart Crawford, Denis Murphy and Colin McKeever all represented, but Gallyhill – who donned the familiar colours of Wilson Dennison – was sent off at odds of 5/1 and looked above average as he ploughed his way through the mud to record a comfortable two-and-a-half-length victory.

Always travelling smoothly in the mid-division, he jumped notably well before edging closer to the pace after a good leap over the third from home. Racing widest of all, he put in a short stride at the penultimate fence before moving into second position on the turn into the bottom part of the track. Quickly back on the bridle, he eased past the leader before taking the bend for home and was kept up to his work in the straight before popping over the last. Pushed out to the line, he held the vastly experienced Ballybegg – also owned by Dennison – at bay to win by two and a half lengths, with a head back to the third.

Sent to the Cheltenham Sale in December, no one could have predicted the outcome when the hammer dropped to the tune of £450,000 (the second highest figure recorded for a P2P horse sold at public auction behind Flemenshill at £480,000) selling the way of Henrietta Knight, who outbid Gordon Elliott, for Mike Grech.

Knight described Gallyhill in the *Racing Post as* "a lovely horse, an outstanding horse ... I've known all about this horse for a long time, I've followed him right the way through. He is a big horse, but he is so athletic, so light on his feet. He's a very good jumper too."

His dam, Tanit, has produced three successful runners from as many racecourse representatives, including his full brother Avoid De Master and half-brother Nortonthorpelegend trained by Rebecca Menzies.

Set to enter training with Nicky Henderson, obviously all eyes will be firmly upon him when he makes his eagerly awaited debut. I'm sure a winning opportunity will be found for him during his first season, but we won't see the best of him for a few years yet.

Henrietta Knight with plenty of reason to smile having purchased Gallyhill for a sale-topping £450,000 on behalf of Mike Grech (Picture by Tattersalls)

GARS DE SCEAUX
4YO GREY GELDING

TRAINER:	Gordon Elliott
PEDIGREE:	Saddler Maker – Replique (April Night)
FORM (P2P):	1 -
OPTIMUM TRIP:	2m +
GOING:	Soft

☆ **STAR POTENTIAL** ☆

A hugely exciting debut winner with the potential to reach the top grade for Gordon Elliott and J P McManus.

Gars De Sceaux caught the attention of many top judges at Borris House in March where he overcame a serious blunder at the penultimate fence to win the second division of the four-year-old geldings' maiden in a time three seconds quicker than the opening heat.

The scopey son of Saddler Maker always appeared to travel within his comfort zone behind the pacesetters but was momentarily on the back foot after a slow leap over the third from home. Bumped along for a stride, the grey was breathtaking in response and quickly bridged the deficit and gained three places as he rocketed into second position.

Continuing his forward move, he took up the running until a terrible blunder over the penultimate fence surrendered his advantage and almost saw him out of the contest. Somehow finding a leg, the four-year-old wrestled back the advantage before the last, jumping the fence well before powering clear up the run-in for a decisive six-length victory over Magic Tricks.

This truly was a race which made you sit up and take note. It takes a special horse to overcome that sort of a blunder, but to shirk it off in such a manner is indicative of a horse with a huge amount of ability.

Gars De Sceaux comes from the family of Bristol De Mai and is bred by the same breeders responsible for Un De Sceaux.

Not only does he have boundless stamina, he also appears to have copious amounts of speed and should have no problem in bumpers, if connections choose to take that route. I expect he'll be a Festival horse, if not this season, then certainly in years to come.

The potentially very useful Gars De Seaux will carry the colours of J P McManus (Picture by Emma O'Brien)

GARTER LANE
5YO CHESTNUT MARE

TRAINER:	Barry O'Connell
PEDIGREE:	Getaway – Tariana (Revoque)
FORM (P2P):	1 -
OPTIMUM TRIP:	2m +
GOING:	Good to Soft

Garter Lane produced a professional performance on her debut and was snapped up by Gerry Hogan at Cheltenham in November 2019 for £100,000.

The good-looking daughter of Getaway made her debut for Philip Fenton in a 14-runner four-year-old mares' maiden at Lisronagh early last November and had evidently been showing positive signs at home as she was well supported in the betting, eventually going off the 3/1 co-favourite.

Never giving her supporters cause for concern, the chestnut travelled stylishly in the mid-division and made smooth progress bypassing the third from home. Soon on the heels of the leaders, she jumped to the front over the penultimate fence and despite an untidy landing she upped the tempo considerably on the level, readily creating distance between herself and the chasers. Hesitant but safe at the last, her lead was diminished but she kept on gamely under hands and heels riding up the run-in to record a comfortable four-length victory from Always Able with a further five-length break back to the third.

The form doesn't look the strongest but the fifth, Annie Day, has since won and the time Garter Lane recorded was the quickest on the day.

A half-sister to bumper/2m chase winner King Spirit, bumper winner Where Eagles Dare and point winner Wicked Games. Her dam was placed on the Flat over 1m4f and 2m2f. She is a sister to 1m2f-1m4f Flat/2m hurdle winner Time On Your Side out of a 1m and 1m6f winner.

There's plenty of speed in Garter Lane's pedigree which suggests she'll be more effective over a shorter trip where her turn of foot will certainly be an asset.

GERICAULT ROQUE
4YO BAY GELDING

TRAINER:	David Pipe
PEDIGREE:	Montmartre – Nijinska Delaroque (Lute Antique)
FORM (P2P):	4 -
OPTIMUM TRIP:	2m +
GOING:	Soft

This French-bred gelding may slip under the radar.

Gericault Roque started his career in a hotly contested four-year-olds' maiden at Tallow in February, a race which was won by Glenglass who subsequently fetched £155,000 and now enters training with Gordon Elliott.

This gelding, trained by Mary Doyle, stalked the early pace and was working his way into the race at the third from home when badly hampered and brought to a virtual standstill. It was an incident which would have caused a lesser horse to struggle to regather his momentum, but Gericault Roque steadily found his feet and stayed on well over the final two fences to finish just shy of eight lengths adrift of the leading trio.

Without the incident, the four-year-old would almost definitely have played a part in the finish. With this in mind and given how highly the winner is rated, Gericault Roque could go underestimated when he makes his Rules debut.

David Pipe – who has enjoyed plenty of recent success with his purchases from these connections, including Israel Champ and Eden Du Houx – has acquired this gelding privately to run in the colours of Bryan Drew.

The gelding is a half-brother to a French 2m1f chase winner Balou De La Roque. His dam is a French 2m1f chaser winner out of a 1m2f-1m3f Flat/2m1f-2m3f Listed-placed hurdle winner.

This good-bodied sort will likely start in a bumper and should be given the utmost respect.

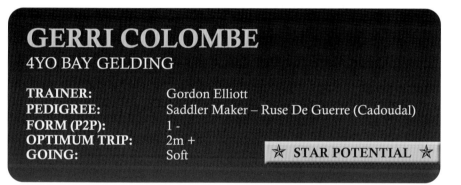

GERRI COLOMBE
4YO BAY GELDING

TRAINER:	Gordon Elliott
PEDIGREE:	Saddler Maker – Ruse De Guerre (Cadoudal)
FORM (P2P):	1 -
OPTIMUM TRIP:	2m +
GOING:	Soft

☆ **STAR POTENTIAL** ☆

Another hugely promising individual to join Gordon Elliott's string.

The athletically built son of Saddler Maker was one of six runners who went to post for the four-year-old geldings' maiden at Lingstown in March where he came away victorious after getting up in the shadows of the post to deny the Denis Murphy-trained Lakota Warrior by a head.

Gerri Colombe, an €85,000 store purchase from the Land Rover Derby Sale in June 2019, travelled kindly in a prominent position under Barry O'Neill and touched down with a narrow advantage over the fourth from home. Joined as the pace increased on the run to the next, he jumped the fence in his stride but was forced wide on the right-hand turn for home and dropped to third position. Pushed along for a stride or two, the gelding responded willingly and cleared two out before quickening on the downhill run to the last. With the two market leaders pulling clear of the field, Gerri Colombe did well to wrestle back the half-length deficit on the run to the line and eventually clung on bravely to win by a head.

With only a few lengths separating the field with two fences to jump, owing to the steady pace, the form is hard to assess. That, however, did not stop Margaret O'Toole shelling out £240,000 for the four-year-old at the Cheltenham Festival Sale in March.

By Saddler Maker out of a Cadoudal mare I would expect the gelding to be seen to best effect when the emphasis is on stamina but there is plenty in his pedigree to suggest he won't be left behind in bumpers or the two-mile hurdle division.

Set to join Gordon Elliott in the colours of Robcour. He is in the right hands to flourish into a decent track performer.

Gerri Colombe - an exciting youngster set to join Gordon Elliott in the colours of Robcour (Picture by Tattersalls)

GLENGLASS
4YO CHESTNUT GELDING

TRAINER:	Gordon Elliott
PEDIGREE:	Ocovango - Funny Times (Silver Patriarch)
FORM (P2P):	1 -
OPTIMUM TRIP:	2m 4f +
GOING:	Soft

Colin Bowe's Glenglass looked a top prospect when producing a resolute performance to win on his debut at Tallow in early February.

Eight runners went to post for what looked a very competitive four-year-olds' maiden, and although this gelding wasn't the most fluent over his fences, he showed a tremendous will to win under Barry O'Neill.

Although the imposing chestnut effortlessly covered the ground with his long-reaching stride, he needed plenty of organising in the jumping department and lacked fluency over the third and fourth from home. Showing plenty of power and a determined attitude, he moved up to the leader's quarters approaching the penultimate fence, but again, was outjumped and was forced to regather his momentum around the home bend.

Lacking nothing in courage, he nosed into the lead once more on the run to the last and overcame one final blunder before galloping bravely to the line to record a one-length victory over Poppa Poutine in a time 16 seconds quicker than the day's average.

This was a strong performance from Glenglass, especially when you consider how much momentum he lost over the final four fences. He evidently has plenty of stamina and the testing conditions suited him well.

The four-year-old is the seventh foal out of the dual-bumper winner Funny Times, herself a sister to Last Of The Bunch who was also successful in a bumper and later went on to win over hurdles up to 2m5f. His immediate family include bumper and 2m4f hurdle winner Flementime, and also Mrs Hyde, a bumper and dual-hurdle winner.

Glenglass has a sizable frame to fill and it will be some time before he realises his true potential. That said, his latent ability should enable him to go well in bumpers or novice hurdles this season, especially on a galloping track where he can really use his stride.

Glenglass has the size and scope to develop into a chaser (Photo by Tattersalls)

GLORY AND HONOUR
4YO BAY GELDING

TRAINER:	TBC
PEDIGREE:	Elusive Pimpernel – On Khee (Sakhee)
FORM (P2P):	1 -
OPTIMUM TRIP:	2m
GOING:	Good to Soft

Glory And Honour was unsold for £58,000 earlier this year, but is certainly one to note wherever he turns up.

The son of Elusive Pimpernel was simply head and shoulders above his competition when making all to win impressively by 15 lengths on his debut in a 2m 4f Open Maiden at Chaddesley Corbett in February.

Ridden by Tommie O'Brien and trained by Anya Ingman, the four-year-old bounced out and jumped particularly well despite the searching pace and was still hard on the bridle approaching the fourth from home.

Allowed a short breather on the run to the next, he got in a little close to the fence but was quickly away and soon pulled five lengths clear of his nearest pursuer turning for home. Not for stopping, the bay continued to motor and extended his advantage before jumping the final two fences efficiently and was nudged home under hands and heels riding to secure victory.

By Elusive Pimpernel out of the Sakhee mare, Oh Khee, Glory And Honour's pedigree certainly has a strong bias towards speed. With that in mind, he should be noted in bumpers but his quick fencing bodes well for a fruitful novice hurdle campaign.

GREENROCK ABBEY
4YO CHESTNUT GELDING

TRAINER:	Alan King
PEDIGREE:	El Salvador – Aos Dana (Fourstars Allstar)
FORM (P2P):	1
OPTIMUM TRIP:	2m +
GOING:	Good to Soft

A flashy distant relative of Beef Or Salmon.

Greenrock Abbey showed himself to be an above average sort when making a winning start to his racing career at Tyrella in March, where he accounted for a well-contested six-runner four-year-olds' maiden run on good ground.

The racy son of El Salvador travelled smoothly behind the pace setters who set a brisk tempo, and he jumped well, especially at the third from home where he spied a stride. Still appearing to have plenty left in the tank on the run to the next, the gelding made a challenge between his rivals on the approach and produced a big leap, gaining him a length in the air before touching down with momentum which he used to pull a couple of lengths clear on the level.

Kept up to his work rounding the bend for home, the gelding delivered one final good jump over the last before running green and idling up the straight which allowed his nearest pursuer to close to within one length crossing the line.

Visually, this was a nice performance from the chestnut, but the time was nothing special which is probably why he was picked up by Highflyer for only

£65,000 at the Cheltenham Festival Sale in March. He has since joined Alan King and will run in the colours of the Million In Mind Partnership.

A half-brother to 2m hurdle winner Stanton Court and bumper winner Eat My Dirt. His dam placed in point-to-points and is a half-sister to the dam responsible for producing Hebridean – a winner on the Flat up to 1m4f, including a Group 3 over 1m2f for Aidan O'Brien before winning a Grade 2 over hurdles for Paul Nicholls.

Greenrook Abbey should be capable in a bumper before being asked to tackle hurdles.

GRIZZMAN
4YO GREY GELDING

TRAINER:	Tom Lacey
PEDIGREE:	Al Namix – Lavi (Evening World)
FORM:	1 – 3
OPTIMUM TRIP:	2m
GOING:	Good to Soft

This Al Namix gelding has plenty more to offer.

Grizzman was purchased privately by Tom Lacey prior to making a winning debut for his wife, Sophie, in a 2m 4f maiden at Larkhill in mid-March. Obviously well-touted beforehand, the four-year-old was sent off the 4/6 favourite under Tommie O'Brien and always raced in a prominent position before moving through to lead at the eleventh fence. From there, the attractive grey made the best of his way home, staying on well in the closing stages to fend off the challenge of Francesca Nimmo's four-year-old, Adjournment, to win by three-quarters of a length.

The collective feeling from spectators was that they'd seen two smart horses pull 25 lengths clear of the remainders.

Grizzman made his bumper debut for Tom at Fontwell in early September where he went off the well-supported favourite under Jonathan Burke. Towering over his opposition, the grey travelled strongly, perhaps a little keenly throughout the race, but couldn't match the turn of foot produced by the eventual winner when the race developed into a sprint up the straight.

Grizzman boasts a speed-biased pedigree. His dam was placed on the Flat in France over 7.5f-9.7f and is a half-sister to a 2m1f-2m2f hurdle/chase winner Tigre out of a Flat 1m2f winner and later 1m7f-2m2f hurdler.

I am inclined to forgive his Rules debut as I don't think he was suited by the tactics of the race. I believe the best is yet to come.

GUARDINO
4YO BROWN GELDING

TRAINER:	Ben Pauling
PEDIGREE:	Authorized – Monicker (Manduro)
FORM (P2P):	2 -
OPTIMUM TRIP:	2m
GOING:	Good to Soft

A Flat-bred gelding who should be noted in bumpers.

Guardino attracted strong market support when making his debut for Denis Murphy in a 2m 4f four-year-old geldings' maiden at Oldtown in February – a race previously won by the likes of Very Wood, and more recently Asterion Forlonge – but he could only manage to clinch second position despite staying on well in the latter stages.

The brown gelding jumped cleanly throughout the race and was asked to bridge the 15-length deficit with the long-time leader on the right-hand turn for home. Doing his best and responding willingly to his rider, Guardino closed to within a few lengths at the last but he was unable to sustain his effort on the short run to the line and was beaten by three and a half lengths.

Given the testing conditions and the ground he was asked to make up turning for home, this was a decent performance by the four-year-old who should be noted in bumpers or the two-mile hurdle division.

Purchased by Highflyer on behalf of Ben Pauling for £170,000 at Cheltenham's February Sale. He is a half-brother to a French 6.5f all-weather winner who attained a mark of 80. His dam was a useful 94-rated 9.5f/10.5f winner out of a 1m 4f Listed winner with the further family linking back to Group 1 winners Getaway and Guadalupe.

Guardino has gone to a yard with an excellent strike-rate with their point-to-point purchases and this looks like another prospect who will do well for them.

HIDDEN COMMANDER
5YO BAY GELDING

TRAINER:	Philip Kirby
PEDIGREE:	Shirocco – Gift Of Freedom (Presenting)
FORM (P2P):	01 -
OPTIMUM TRIP:	2m 4f +
GOING:	Soft

Philip Kirby's string of horses goes from strength to strength and this gelding looks another useful addition.

Hidden Commander failed to show a great deal on his debut for Mary Doyle at Lingstown in November 2019 but got off the mark at the second time of asking when sticking on gamely to claim a five-year-old geldings' maiden at Borris House at the beginning of March.

Having been patiently ridden by Aaron Sinnott, the gelding made a notable forward move after the fourth from home and went into second before setting his sights on the long-time leader. Pulling clear of the third but still 10 lengths adrift of the front runner, the gelding responded well to urgings after a good leap over the third from home and closed to within a few lengths by the time they had reached the penultimate fence.

Staying on dourly and showing a good attitude on the short run to the last, the son of Shirocco met the final fence on a long stride and despite going through the top of the birch he landed with momentum which he used to overhaul Flame Bearer on the run-in, eventually crossing the line one length to the good with a distance back to the 2/1 favourite, Pay The Piper, in third.

Following the race James Doyle – brother of the winning trainer – said, "He is a lovely horse and we have thought plenty of him; we will just have to draw a line through the first run. He jumps and did the business for Aaron today."

Led out of the ring unsold for £48,000 at the Cheltenham Festival Sale in March, he has since been purchased privately and now resides at Green Oaks in North Yorkshire.

A half-brother to last season's Irish Paddy Power Chase winner, Roaring Bull. His further family link back to the smart chaser, Jessies Dream.

There's plenty to like about Hidden Commander. By Shirocco out of a Presenting mare, it wouldn't be a surprise to see him show up well in a bumper, but I expect he'll excel once his stamina is tested.

HOLLOW GAMES
4YO BAY GELDING

TRAINER:	Gordon Elliott
PEDIGREE:	Beat Hollow – I'm Grand (Raise A Grand)
FORM (P2P):	1 -
OPTIMUM TRIP:	2m +
GOING:	Soft

★ **STAR POTENTIAL** ★

A hugely impressive winner with a bright future ahead of him.

Hollow Games made his debut in a four-year-old geldings' maiden at Turtulla in March and was one of only two finishers from the eight-strong line-up to complete the three-mile contest run on ground officially described as soft/heavy.

The son of Beat Hollow always moved powerfully in a prominent position and still appeared to be travelling well within his comfort zone after jumping the fifth from home. Continuing to track the leader, he again came up well at the next fence and moved alongside the leader as the pair drew clear of the field around the sweeping bend for home.

Shaken up on the landing side of the third from home, the four-year-old lengthened his stride and edged into a narrow advantage before producing a good leap over the penultimate fence where his nearest pursuer made a race-ending blunder. Left a long way clear of the remainder, he continued to power down to the last, meeting it on a good stride before lengthening to the line to record an impressive success.

Hollow Games looks an imposing individual and produced a lovely round of jumping despite the testing conditions. He also showed a good deal of stamina to always be up with the pace before picking off the leader and powering away to the line.

Out of a half-sister to the Grade 2-winning chaser Tumbling Dice and from the family of the high-class chaser Remittance Man. This smart-looking individual was purchased from the Cheltenham Festival Sale in March for £255,000 by Aidan O'Ryan acting on behalf of Gordon Elliott and will now run in the colours of Noel Moran, who sponsors Elliott's yard.

He looks a smart sort with the potential to reach the top grade. Given his imposing physique, connections may kick on with him over hurdles, but he should be noted wherever he starts.

HOLYMACAPONY
4YO BAY GELDING

TRAINER:	TBC
PEDIGREE:	Libertarian – Heavenly Star (King's Theatre)
FORM (P2P):	1 -
OPTIMUM TRIP:	2m 4f +
GOING:	Soft

Holymacapony provided Libertarian with his first four-year-old point winner when making most to win on his debut at Kirkistown in February.

The Cormac Farrell-trained gelding bounded to the front as the flag went up and set a strong even gallop throughout the three-mile contest. His jumping was occasionally patchy but he gained ground with two bold leaps over the fourth and third from home before losing his position when getting in tight to the penultimate fence.

Driven on the landing side, the bay took time to regather his momentum but was able to re-establish his position on the turn out of the back straight before kicking on again down the side of the track. Strongly ridden and hard pressed on the long run to the last, he kept finding for Simon Cavanagh and popped over the fence neatly before staying on powerfully to win by seven lengths from Grady Hollow, clocking a time 12 seconds quicker than the day's average.

Following the race his handler said, "This is a lovely horse; he is a real athlete. He stays all day and I think he has a big future because he is still a big raw baby. I think he can go on to much better things."

From the family of Wayward Lad, this home-bred gelding looks to have a nice blend of speed and stamina. He also has a very willing attitude which is sure to stand him in good stead in future.

HOME FARM HOUSE
5YO BLACK MARE

TRAINER:	David Pipe
PEDIGREE:	Winged Love – Recession Lass (Presenting)
FORM (P2P):	1 -
OPTIMUM TRIP:	2m 4f
GOING:	Good to Soft

Home Farm House looks a gutsy individual and should be capable in the mares' division for her new connections.

The Kieran Roche-trained mare made her debut a winning one at Knockmullen House in early February where the ground was officially described as soft. Benefiting from a good ride by James Walsh, the five-year-old was held up in the mid-division and made steady progress into fourth position at the fourth from home. A little slow over the next, she was pushed along for a couple of strides but picked up nicely to regain her position before moving into third on the uphill part of the track.

Ridden to challenge approaching the penultimate fence, the mare responded generously and comprehensively outjumped her nearest pursuer before stretching a couple of lengths clear on the run to the last. A bad mistake there almost had her on the ground, but she had plenty left in the tank to pick herself up and galloped strongly to the line.

The pace was slow and it didn't look the deepest of contests, but considering this was Home Farm House's debut, it was a nice performance and the form received a boost when the third – beaten five lengths – went on to be a close second next time.

Picked up cheaply from the Cheltenham Sale in February by Tom Malone for £24,000, Home Farm House is a full sister to a point winner and will most likely be suited to intermediate trips on good ground.

She's not the biggest individual but David Pipe does well with his point-to-point purchases and I'm sure there'll be races for her.

INDIGO BREEZE
4YO BAY/BROWN GELDING

TRAINER: TBC
PEDIGREE: Martaline – Miss Poutine (Chamberlin)
FORM (P2P): 1 -
OPTIMUM TRIP: 2m +
GOING: Soft

A useful-looking half-brother to Brindisi Breeze.

Indigo Breeze justified short odds to win a point-to-point bumper at Alnwick in March by a very easy 25 lengths. It was one-way traffic from the drop of the flag as Jack Andrews guided the Gearoid Costelloe-trained gelding from the front and quickened into an unassailable lead over half a mile from home.

The form looks good with the second, Simplystic, showing plenty of ability and looking the likely winner of a Sedgefield bumper for Mark Walford until appearing to go amiss inside the final two furlongs.

Purchased for €90,000 from the Derby Store Sale in Ireland in June 2019. He has since passed through the ring at Cheltenham following his victory but was led out unsold for £140,000.

I'm unsure of the gelding's whereabouts, but this well-bred sort should be more than capable of winning a bumper before embarking on a career over hurdles. He could be a very useful prospect for his new connections.

Indigo Breeze (Photo by Tattersalls)

KILBEG KING
5YO BAY GELDING

TRAINER:	TBC
PEDIGREE:	Doyen – Prayuwin Drummer (Presenting)
FORM (P2P):	2 -
OPTIMUM TRIP:	2m +
GOING:	Good to Soft

Kilbeg King looks to have plenty more to offer.

The five-year-old Doyen gelding made his debut in an ordinary maiden at Tinahely in January where he looked the likely winner until fluffing his lines at the final fence. Trained by Colin Bowe and ridden by Barry O'Neill, the bay moved well throughout the three-mile contest and edged closer to the pace at the fourth from home. Still travelling on the bridle, he took aim at the leader when going out of camera view but emerged back into sight at the top of the hill with a slender advantage.

Ridden to assert after jumping the penultimate fence, he responded well, pulling a couple of lengths clear before misjudging his stride at the final fence. Landing flat-footed and losing momentum, the door opened for the more experienced Folcano, who jumped to the lead and showed a greater acceleration away from the fence to win by a length and a half.

Without the final fence mishap, Kilbeg King would almost certainly have gone on to win. The way he regathered his momentum to pull clear of the third suggested he had plenty left in the tank.

Withdrawn from a couple of the spring sales, I am unsure of his whereabouts, but he is certainly one to look out for. He looks to possess a useful blend of speed and stamina.

KILLER KANE
5YO BAY GELDING

TRAINER:	Colin Tizzard
PEDIGREE:	Oscar – Native Idea (Be My Native)
FORM (P2P):	1 -
OPTIMUM TRIP:	2m 4f +
GOING:	Good to Soft

Killer Kane looks like another Saturday horse for Colin Tizzard.

This well-related half-brother to the 2009 Grade 1 Supreme Novices' Hurdle winner, Go Native, got off the mark at the first time of asking in a six-runner five-year-old geldings' maiden at Ballycahane in March.

Trained by Donnchadh Doyle and partnered by Rob James, the Oscar gelding tracked the leader for the main part of the race and always moved stylishly. Jumping boldly, if not a little big at times, a half-length separated him from the pacesetter after the fourth from home and he continued to hold that position over the next before taking aim over the penultimate fence. He was a little sticky there, but his jockey took a glance over his shoulder upon touching down before letting out an inch of rein which allowed Killer Kane to take up the running.

Quickening the tempo as they straightened up for home, the five-year-old hung slightly, but lengthened into a two-length lead approaching the final fence, which he took in his stride before readily asserting on the run to the line to win by three lengths from the staying on Fabrique En France.

Killer Kane looks an imposing sort and it's testament to his natural ability that he was able to not only win, but to show a turn of foot off the slow pace.

Bred to be smart, it's not surprising he topped the Cheltenham Festival Sale in March, selling the way of Peter & Ross Doyle Bloodstock on behalf of Colin Tizzard for £300,000.

Given his age and size, I would imagine connections will be keen to press on with him over hurdles.

LAKOTA WARRIOR
4YO BROWN GELDING

TRAINER:	Dan Skelton
PEDIGREE:	Valirann – Talkin Madam (Talkin Man)
FORM (P2P):	2 -
OPTIMUM TRIP:	2m +
GOING:	Good to Soft

☆ **STAR POTENTIAL** ☆

Lakota Warrior bumped into the smart Gerri Colombe on his debut at Lingstown in March but highlighted himself as a horse to follow despite coming off second best.

The Denis Murphy-trained gelding is a fine, classy-looking individual, who travelled stylishly towards the rear of the tightly grouped six-runner field. Jumping professionally, he produced a good leap over the fourth from home taking him into a share of third position, but Jamie Codd was happy to wait a little longer and restrained his mount on the long run to the next.

Again, he jumped the fence in his stride and continued to travel strongly on the wide outside before making a notable move on the approach to two out. Quickening into the wings of the fence, he came up well and landed in second spot before moving into a narrow advantage on the downhill part of the track. Locking horns with the eventual winner, the pair were stride for stride as they accelerated to the last and although they took off together, this gelding touched down with a slender lead, but he couldn't quite hold on to the line and lost out by a head.

Lakota Warrior did very little wrong in defeat. He travelled smoothly, jumped very well and Jamie Codd produced him at the right time. Perhaps the ground he conceded by travelling wide into the straight was the difference between winning and losing.

The €58,000 store purchase is a half-brother to the very useful bumper/2m4f and 3m hurdle winner Run Wild Fred. His dam was a maiden point winner and a half-sister to 2m3f-2m5f hurdle/chase winner McIlhatton and 2m4f chase/3m hurdle winner Well Saved.

Not sold for £145,000 earlier this year at the Cheltenham Festival Sale, he has since joined Dan Skelton.

LESSER
6YO BAY GELDING

TRAINER:	Richard Phillips
PEDIGREE:	Stowaway – Aine Dubh (Bob Back)
FORM (P2P):	1 -
OPTIMUM TRIP:	2m 4f +
GOING:	Good to Soft

Richard Phillips does well with the horses which come his way, and although Lesser may not prove to be a world-beater, he should pay his way.

The six-year-old son of Stowaway made a belated start to his career in a maiden at Ballycrystal where he made light work of the 10-runner field to win by an easy six lengths in a good time.

Delivered from off the pace by the five-pound claimer Conor Blake, the gelding arrived on to the scene down the far side of the track, jumping four from home in a share of fourth place before pressing for the lead on the run to the next. Nudged along rounding the turn for home, the gelding moved into a narrow lead over the penultimate fence and pulled clear under hands and heels riding before another spring-heeled leap over the last propelled him to the line.

The race looked nothing more than ordinary but the third, who finished 11 lengths adrift, offers some substance after winning by 10 lengths on his next start.

A full brother to 2m7f-3m1f hurdle winner Triopas, and a half-brother to the four-time winner Dubh Eile, out of the useful Graded-placed Aine Dubh, from the family of the high-class hurdler Mighty Mogul.

Bought for £50,000 at Cheltenham in January, there should be plenty of fun to be had with Lesser, especially when the emphasis is on stamina.

LETS GO CHAMP
5YO BAY GELDING

TRAINER:	Tom George
PEDIGREE:	Jeremy – Dark Mimosa (Bahri)
FORM (P2P):	1 -
OPTIMUM TRIP:	2m
GOING:	Good

Lets Go Champ missed last season having suffered a setback after joining Tom George but I fully expect him to make up for lost time this term.

The attractive gelding looked well above average when digging deep on his debut at Bartlemy in May 2019 and was subsequently sold to Roger Brookhouse for £375,000 at Doncaster later that month.

Sent off the evens favourite of the 10-runner maiden, Rob James always oozed confidence aboard the four-year-old as they tracked the pace in the early stages of the race. A forward move was made on the long run to three from home and Lets Go Champ significantly upped the tempo before producing a foot-perfect leap over the fence.

Pressing on when taking the tight bend for home, he continued to accelerate down to the penultimate fence, which he gave very little respect, but he got away with it and continued to gallop on three lengths clear of the field. That gap was diminished by Full Back at the last who produced a good leap to challenge but Lets Go Champ found extra on the run-in to win by a cosy one and a quarter lengths with a break of 10 lengths back to the third.

Lets Go Champ was tying up a little close home, not helped by his mistake at the last, but he is bred to be suited to trips much sharper than this and so it's credit to his ability that he was able to hold the stoutly bred runner-up at the line.

By Jeremy out of a Bahri mare, the bay is a three-parts brother to Our Conor and a full brother to Joseph O'Brien's bumper winner Scarlet And Dove.

This is a quick sort and I fully expect him to put his potent turn of foot to good use in bumpers.

LONG STAY
5YO BAY GELDING

TRAINER:	Fergal O'Brien
PEDIGREE:	Nathaniel – Mainstay (Elmaamul)
FORM:	62F - 1
OPTIMUM TRIP:	2m
GOING:	Soft

This well-bred Nathaniel gelding showed a modicum of promise on his three starts in the pointing field for Denis Hogan and is a very interesting acquisition for Fergal O'Brien.

Long Stay was beaten 25 lengths into sixth position on his debut in testing conditions at Loughrea in October 2019, but took a step forward a month later at Dromahane where he finished six lengths adrift of Sleepysaurus – staying on dourly for pressure despite being badly hampered and losing ground at the fourth from home in a race which clocked a time 18 seconds faster than the day's average.

Sent off the 5/2 favourite in what looked a stronger contest at Tattersalls Farm in December, he again showed hints of potential but lost his position after clouting the third from home and eventually took a tired fall at the last when weakening well out of contention.

Since joining his new connections, he has already shown he has plenty of ability by winning a bumper at Newton Abbot by nine lengths. The manner with which he travelled before putting the race to bed suggested he has plenty more to offer, which is why I am leaving him in this book.

This well-bred individual is a half-brother to the 116-rated 7f Group 2 winner Richard Pankhurst, the 112-rated 7f Group 3 winner Crazy Horse and 8.5f winner Millicent Fawcett. His dam was an 84-rated 1m winner who is a half-sister to 1m1f Group 3-winner Lateen Sails out of a 6f two-year-old winner.

He should have no problem following up under a penalty before switching to hurdles.

MAGGIES MOGUL
4YR BAY FILLY

TRAINER:	David Pipe
PEDIGREE:	Valirann – Grangeclare Gold (Old Vic)
FORM (P2P):	1 -
OPTIMUM TRIP:	2m 4f +
GOING:	Soft

★ **STAR POTENTIAL** ★

A really likeable mare blessed with the will to win.

Colin Bowe's daughter of Valirann was unrelenting on the front end when making every yard a winning one under Barry O'Neill on her debut at Ballyarthur in March, displaying a hugely commendable attitude and a fully accomplished round of jumping to cross the line two lengths clear of Flames Of Passion with a 15-length break back to the third.

The mare looked head and shoulders above the field from a very early stage and bounded up the hill to the third from home with her ears pricked. Stretching her lead and quickening the tempo approaching the last, she then demonstrated to have plenty left in the tank when repelling the challenge of Flames Of Passion who came from off the pace under Jamie Codd. One final quick leap left the race in no doubt as she kept on willingly under hands and heels riding to the line.

This well-made mare is out of a half-sister to the high-class Real Steel. She is also a half-sister to bumper winner Laoch Liam, and bumper/2m2f/2m3f hurdle winner, Little Nugget. The further family include Scarthy Lad and Grangeclare Lark.

Purchased privately, she is now in the care of David Pipe at Pond House.

Maggies Mogul looks a top prospect and should have no problem dropping back in trip to tackle a bumper, although I expect her to flourish over obstacles and later fences when her stamina comes into play.

MAGIC TRICKS
4YO BAY GELDING

TRAINER:	Gordon Elliott
PEDIGREE:	Davidoff – Cadoubelle Des As (Cadoudal)
FORM (P2P):	2 -
OPTIMUM TRIP:	2m +
GOING:	Soft

☆ **STAR POTENTIAL** ☆

A full brother to the talented Abacadabras.

This exciting individual finished second to another high-class sort when lining up in a quality four-year-olds' maiden at Borris House at the beginning of March – a race won 12 months ago by Sporting John.

Never too far off the pace, Magic Tricks jumped well and held a narrow advantage over the fourth from home but dropped to third with a sticky leap over the next. Quickly reasserting to the head of the field after being pushed along for a stride, the bay moved into a length advantage but was tracked all the while by Gars De Sceaux who loomed up to challenge around the home bend and moved to the front over the penultimate fence despite a bad error.

Magic Tricks did his best to rally, but couldn't match the pace produced by the eventual winner between the final two fences and had to settle for the runner-up spot, six lengths behind Jamie Codd's mount with the same distance back to the third, Zoom Zoom Zoe who has since showed a useful level of ability in the States.

Purchased privately since his debut, the son of Davidoff now finds himself in the care of Gordon Elliott in the colours of J P McManus.

With a pedigree biased towards speed and from a talented family, you would have to be confident that Magic Tricks can get off the mark with the minimal amount of fuss under Rules.

Gordon Elliott has a tremendous team of horses to look forward to (Picture by Tattersalls)

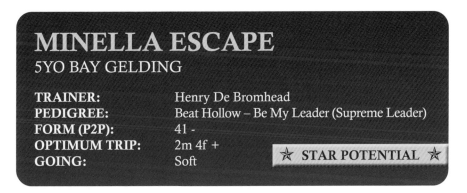

MINELLA ESCAPE
5YO BAY GELDING

TRAINER:	Henry De Bromhead
PEDIGREE:	Beat Hollow – Be My Leader (Supreme Leader)
FORM (P2P):	41 -
OPTIMUM TRIP:	2m 4f +
GOING:	Soft

☆ **STAR POTENTIAL** ☆

A strong-travelling gelding with plenty of scope to develop into a chaser.

Minella Escape was well supported and showed plenty of potential to finish fourth on his debut at Boulta in December, but perhaps lacked fitness as his stamina gave way following a slight mistake at the third from home.

Given time to freshen up, he was next seen at the picturesque Bellharbour in February where he clearly benefited from his experience to return the convincing winner of the five-year-old geldings' maiden, previously won by Mall Dini and Joseph O'Brien's expensive purchase, Dlauro.

The race was run at a strong pace and the Beat Hollow gelding was always well positioned behind the leader before moving up to challenge at the fourth from home. Continuing to move powerfully, he took to the front with a quick leap over the next and held that position on the short run to the penultimate fence. Quickening on the downhill run for home, he pulled clear of the field and found plenty for gentle pressure before producing a great leap at the last which propelled him up the run-in to win by an easy six lengths from the more experienced Here We Have It.

This was a really good performance from the winner. His quick jumping and the ability to accelerate off the turn for home was impressive, and he had plenty of stamina in reserve for the short uphill climb to the line.

Closely related to Dashing Oscar, a bumper/2m-2m3f hurdle winner, and Judkin, a point/bumper winner. His dam was a bumper/2m4f hurdle/2m6f chase winner and is a half-sister to the eight-time winner, Keepitsecret.

Purchased by Kevin Ross Bloodstock for £100,000, there should be plenty of good days ahead for Minella Escape. He may be seen to best effect on softer ground due to his round knee action.

MINELLA MAJESTIC
5YO BAY GELDING

TRAINER:	TBC
PEDIGREE:	Shantou – Classic Lin (Linamix)
FORM (P2P):	1 -
OPTIMUM TRIP:	2m +
GOING:	Good to Soft

John Nallen's gelding reportedly took the eye in the paddock before embarking on his debut in an 11-runner maiden at Ballindenisk in early December.

Described as an embryonic chaser, Minella Majestic got into a lovely rhythm up with the pace for John Barry and still held a narrow advantage after jumping the third from home. Upping the tempo as the field went out of sight on the long run to two out, the five-year-old emerged with a commanding five-length advantage and jumped the fence well and seemingly had the race in safekeeping heading to the last. Another safe jump there appeared to seal the deal, but his advantage was rapidly diminished on the run to the line as Noble Yeats finished with a wet sail and closed to within a neck.

Minella Majestic understandably looked a little lonely over the final couple of fences but got the job done, with the front two finishing a healthy six lengths clear of the third, Easter In Milan, who was benefiting from experience. The fourth, Bourbon Street, offers a little substance to the form by finishing second twice since, whilst the tenth, Cailin Dearg went on to be second to subsequent bumper winner Nada To Prada, before getting off the mark at Bandon in March.

Minella Majestic is a half-brother to Noel Meade's Grade 3 novice hurdle winner Corbally Ghost (bumper/useful 2m4f/3m hurdle winner), 7f-1m4f Flat/2m hurdle winner Goal and 2m4f chase winner In Your Shadow. His dam is out of a 5f-6f 2yo winner.

With a pedigree littered with speed and stamina, Minella Majestic has the potential to be effective over a range of trips. He certainly looks pacy enough for two miles, but his stature may see him develop into more of a stayer.

ONLY THE BOLD
5YO BAY GELDING

TRAINER:	Evan Williams
PEDIGREE:	Jeremy – Cloghoge Lady (Presenting)
FORM (P2P):	U1 -
OPTIMUM TRIP:	2m +
GOING:	Good

Purchased at Cheltenham's February Sale by Evan Williams for £215,000.

Only The Bold unshipped his jockey at the sixth from home on his debut at Borris House in December but quickly atoned for that error by winning easily the following month at Tyrella.

The sharp County Down track suited this speedy son of Jeremy who helped set the early pace before being left with a narrow advantage at the fourth from home. Travelling powerfully, the five-year-old was then hassled by a loose horse on the run to the next but managed to pull a few lengths clear of the field and produced a spring-heeled leap to carry him further ahead.

Continuing to bound along with ears pricked, he showed no signs of stopping as he led the field into the straight but was kept up to his work approaching the last. Quickening into the wings of the fence, he produced one final excellent leap before motoring clear up the run-in to record an easy nine-length victory over Tommy's Oscar.

In behind were All The Best, who finished fifth on his debut, beaten a little over nine lengths by Gallyhill, and also The Dara Man, who was third on his debut to Askinvillar. Both of those horses offer some substance to the form.

Only The Bold is a half-brother to Willie Mullins' very useful mare, Westerner Lady, a 10-times winner including twice at Grade 3 level. He is also a half-brother to bumper/2m and 2m4f hurdle winner Sapphire Lady, also trained by Willie Mullins. His dam won a bumper and was placed over hurdles.

I liked the way Only The Bold went through his race. He looks to have a fine blend of speed and stamina and will most likely be suited to good ground. He could gain some experience in a bumper before being sent over hurdles.

ORBYS LEGEND
4YO BAY GELDING

TRAINER:	Philip Hobbs
PEDIGREE:	Milan – Morning Legend (Bob Back)
FORM (P2P):	2 -
OPTIMUM TRIP:	2m +
GOING:	Soft

Orbys Legend highlighted himself as a horse to follow when finishing second on his debut in a 2m 4f four-year-olds' maiden at Knockmullen House in February.

The scopey son of Milan was never too far off the pace where he travelled enthusiastically for Harley Dunne before taking up the running with a bold leap over the fourth from home. Continuing to bound along, he spied a stride approaching three out and again came up out of his jockey's hands, gaining a length in the air before stretching the field as he upped the tempo.

Pestered by Brooksway Fair on the steep incline leading to the turn for home, he was ridden off the bend but responded gamely, forging a length clear on the run to the penultimate fence before producing another good leap which helped him get away quickly. Asked to keep up the gallop on the run to the last, he knuckled down bravely but was joined in the air by the eventual winner and didn't quite have the legs to go with him on the run to the line.

This race was a true test of stamina with only two of the 10 starters able to make it to the finish. Orbys Legend did very little wrong in defeat and perhaps paid the price for being up with the pace throughout. By contrast the winner was given a more patient ride and came from the rear.

A full brother to the Jonjo O'Neill-trained Morning Spirit, who showed promise in a couple of novice hurdles last term. His dam is a half-sister to useful bumper/2m-3m1f hurdle/chase winner Morning Royalty, bumper/ smart 2m-2m2f hurdle winner Morning Run and useful bumper/2m-2m4f hurdle/chase winner Morning Supreme.

Orbys Legend's pedigree suggests he should be competitive if tackling a bumper but on the visual evidence to hand, he looks a stayer who has the scope to develop into a chaser.

PATROCLUS
4YO BAY GELDING

TRAINER:	Nicky Henderson
PEDIGREE:	Shirocco – King'sandqueen's (King's Theatre)
FORM (P2P):	2 -
OPTIMUM TRIP:	2m +
GOING:	Soft

The Michael Goff-trained gelding showed plenty of potential on his debut at Ballycahane in March where he travelled strongly in the midfield and jumped well to finish a promising second to Docpickedme.

The son of Shirocco caught the eye throughout the race and edged closer upon touching down after the third from home. Latching himself on to the leading trio, the gelding looked a major threat and continued to advance through the field, jumping himself into third place over the penultimate fence before quickening around the turn for home.

Ridden to take the lead on the level, the gelding had the measure of the horse in front of him but was passed by Docpickedme who came from off the pace and jumped to the front over the final fence. Doing his best to stage a rally, Patroclus showed a good attitude but didn't have the momentum of the eventual winner who went on to win by a length.

There was plenty to like about this performance and the four-year-old proved himself a strong traveller with a turn of foot. I also liked the way he knuckled down after the last and didn't sway from battle all the way to the line.

Purchased as a three-year-old for €28,000 by George Blackborn, he made a healthy return on his investment when selling the way of Highflyer Bloodstock at the Cheltenham Festival Sale for £150,000.

With a pedigree that has both speed and stamina there should be plenty of winning opportunities for Patroclus.

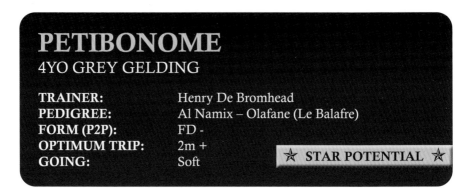

PETIBONOME
4YO GREY GELDING

TRAINER:	Henry De Bromhead
PEDIGREE:	Al Namix – Olafane (Le Balafre)
FORM (P2P):	FD -
OPTIMUM TRIP:	2m +
GOING:	Soft

☆ **STAR POTENTIAL** ☆

Petibonome is a name to note in the colours of Robcour.

The Pat Doyle-trained gelding started his career in a four-year-olds' maiden at Bellharbour in February – a race his Tipperary handler had won six times in the past decade – and was travelling strongly up with the pace until crashing out at the fifth from home.

Given a month to recover, the fall obviously left no lasting effects as the grey then went to Lismore and returned an easy 12-length winner of the eight-runner contest, only to be disqualified for taking the wrong course after the second from home. Despite losing the race, the visual impression was impressive, with the French-bred highlighting himself as a horse with a huge amount of ability, demonstrating a clean round of jumping and plenty of pace to pull clear of the field of newcomers.

Dam is a French 2m hurdle winner and a half-sister to the useful 2m-3m hurdle winner Tanerko Emery. Petibonome now enters training with Henry De Bromhead having been purchased privately.

Blessed with abundant stamina and the ability to quicken off a strong tempo; I like the way the gelding travels with purpose. He oozes class and I have high hopes for him reaching a decent level under Rules.

POPPA POUTINE
4YO BAY GELDING

TRAINER:	Nigel Twiston-Davies
PEDIGREE:	Sholokhov – Sherchanceit (Norwich)
FORM (P2P):	2 -
OPTIMUM TRIP:	3m
GOING:	Good to Soft

Poppa Poutine lost little in defeat when finishing a solid second to Glenglass on his debut at Tallow and looks capable of going one better under Rules.

Given a patient ride by Simon Cavanagh, the good-looking son of Sholokhov made smooth progress from mid-division on the final circuit before being nudged along to improve his position further after the fourth from home. As the bay moved closer to the pace, he was lucky to avoid the drama on the landing side of three out but responded well to further urgings on the bend for home before losing momentum when getting in close to the penultimate fence whilst challenging for second position.

Firmly driven on the landing side, to the gelding's great credit he dug deep to claw back the two-length deficit before the last and produced a good leap which propelled him into second spot up the run-in to cross the line a length behind the winner.

Purchased as a three-year-old at the prestigious Derby Sale in Ireland for €40,000, he realised a healthy profit when selling to Ian Ferguson for £100,000 at Cheltenham's February Sale and now finds himself in the care of Nigel Twiston-Davies.

By Sholokhov out of a Norwich mare, I would expect Poppa Poutine to excel in races which bring his stamina in to play. His half-brother, Northofthewall, was a useful 2m-2m4f hurdler whilst his dam – a 2m1f hurdle winner – is a half-sister to 3m6f/4m1f chase winner, Laundry Lady's Lad.

POZO EMERY
5YO BAY GELDING

TRAINER:	Paul Nicholls
PEDIGREE:	Le Havre – Chic Et Zen (Chichicastenango)
FORM (P2P):	2 -
OPTIMUM TRIP:	2m +
GOING:	Good to Soft

Pozo Emery highlighted himself as a name to follow when finishing second to the potentially very useful Reality Cheque in a strongly run five-year-olds' maiden at Kilfeacle in January.

The Le Havre gelding travelled smoothly on the business end under Derek O'Connor and often produced quick, fluent leaps over his fences which ensured he landed with momentum. Still on the bridle after the third from home, the gelding gradually upped the tempo and although he got in tight to the penultimate fence, he injected further pace into the race on the long climb to the last. Despite pulling readily clear alongside the eventual winner, he had no more to offer when Reality Cheque quickened up the home straight, but he kept on well to be a distance clear of the only other finisher.

With a pedigree littered with Flat blood, Pozo Emery did well to show promise over a trip which was probably too far, especially considering he was up with the strong pace throughout.

A half-brother to French 11.5f winner Scala Emery, his dam is a French 14.5f winner and a half-sister to French 2m 6f Grade 1 chaser Top Of The Sky.

Set to embark on his Rules career for Paul Nicholls in the colours of The Stewart Family. Pozo Emery wouldn't be out of place in a bumper, but given his fluent fencing, he could make an impact over hurdles before embarking on a chasing career next term.

REALITY CHEQUE
5YO BAY GELDING

TRAINER:	Willie Mullins
PEDIGREE:	Getaway – Coolaghmore Yeats (Yeats)
FORM (P2P):	F1 -
OPTIMUM TRIP:	2m +
GOING:	Soft

☆ **STAR POTENTIAL** ☆

Reality Cheque was an early casualty on his debut at Dromahane in December but left that disappointment behind him when getting off the mark a month later.

The Getaway gelding looked superior in quality against the nine others he lined up against in the five-year-olds' maiden at Kilfeacle. Always travelling with eye-catching ease in the mid-division, he moved on to the heels of the leaders after effortlessly jumping the third from home and eased into second place with another fluent leap over the next.

Pulling clear of the field on the bridle alongside Pozo Emery, he quickened smartly into the wings of the final fence and rapidly sealed the race with a surge of speed up the run-in to win by five lengths.

This was a strongly run contest which clocked the fastest time of the day by a considerable margin, further highlighting the winner as a potentially useful sort.

Reality Cheque is a half-brother to a bumper winner. His dam was unraced but is closely related to the 2m4f/2m5f chase winner and 2m4f hurdle winner Oscar Brunel.

Purchased privately since his success, he is now with Willie Mullins and must be followed closely wherever he lines up. He could be a high-class recruit with his ability to both quicken and stay a trip.

RECITE A PRAYER
5YO BAY GELDING

TRAINER:	TBC
PEDIGREE:	Recital – Old Madam (Old Vic)
FORM (P2P):	P1 -
OPTIMUM TRIP:	3m
GOING:	Soft

Recite A Prayer looks capable of winning his fair share of races when the emphasis is on stamina.

Michael Murphy's gelding scoped badly following a disappointing debut at Dromahane in December when connections were expecting a bold show, but he atoned for that by winning as he liked when sent to Tallow in February.

Never too far off the pace, the imposing sort jumped safely and took advantage of being left in front at the third from home. Galloping on relentlessly in the conditions, the bay had plenty left in reserve when challenged before the penultimate fence and pulled away effortlessly on the run to the last, splashing through the puddles to record an easy 12-length win from the only other finisher, Sunset West.

That horse has since franked the form by filling the runner-up spot on his next start before getting off the mark at Lingstown in March and has subsequently joined Joseph O'Brien. The time of the race also compares favourably to the rest of the card and was only three seconds slower than the opening four-year-olds' maiden which was won by the highly regarded Glenglass.

From the family of Michael Dickinson's three-time Queen Mother Champion Chase winner, Badsworth Boy.

Stamina looks Recite A Prayer's primary asset.

RED BUCCANEER
5YO CHESTNUT GELDING

TRAINER:	Henry Daly
PEDIGREE:	Black Sam Bellamy – Florarossa (Alflora)
FORM (P2P):	2 -
OPTIMUM TRIP:	2m 4f +
GOING:	Good to Soft

This individual is the epitome of an embryonic chaser.

Red Buccaneer, who stands at over 17 hands tall was patiently handled in his early days by Francesca Nimmo, allowing him time to physically develop before embarking on his racing career in January earlier this year.

Making his debut at Larkhill, the imposing chestnut lined up in a 14-runner maiden and was sent off the 3/1 joint favourite under James King. He jumped brilliantly up with the pace and was still comfortably holding his position over the open ditch, three from home. Another bold leap two out pulled him clear of the third but the eventual winner quickened into a length advantage around the home bend and produced a better leap over the final fence which gave her momentum to maintain her lead to the line.

This was a promising debut from Red Buccaneer and the time of the race was favourable in comparison to the first division. The form also received a boost when the winner – who had already won six times – went on to score again.

Red Buccaneer is a half-brother to the 2m hurdle winner Floral Bouquet, and his dam was placed in a bumper. The further family link back to 10-time hurdle winner (including Listed) and three-time chase winner Bayrouge.

Purchased for £35,000 by Andrew Jones, the chestnut will now enter training with Henry Daly.

Given the horse's size, I fully expect him to require plenty of time to reach his full potential.

This season will be all about gaining experience.

Henry Daly has an exciting prospect on his hands with the imposing Red Buccaneer (Photo by Julie Drewett from racehorsephotos.com)

RED LION LAD
4YO BAY GELDING

TRAINER:	David Pipe
PEDIGREE:	Flemensfirth – Hotline (Poliglote)
FORM (P2P):	1 -
OPTIMUM TRIP:	2m +
GOING:	Good to Soft

Red Lion Lad boasts a serious pedigree being out of a Listed-winning half-sister to the dual Queen Mother Champion Chase winner Master Minded.

The well-bred sort made his debut for Colin Bowe and Barry O'Neill in March at Ballyarthur where only seven runners went to post for the four-year-old geldings' maiden which was run on ground officially described as soft/heavy.

Always positioned close to the pace, the gelding was quick through the air over the fourth from home but raced a little awkwardly on the uphill run to the next and for a split second looked as if he may attempt to run out. After getting over safely, he showed good tactical pace to move up to press for the lead on the run to the penultimate fence but a mistake put him on the back foot and he was pushed along in third on the downhill run before the home bend.

Ridden along but given time to find his stride, the bay responded gamely and soon challenged for the lead as they approached the final fence and despite looking a little ponderous, he got over safely and extended impressively on the run-in to win by 10 lengths.

Red Lion Lad showed plenty of immaturity during the race, but I loved his genuine head carriage and the greenness bodes well for future improvement. The time of the race was also favourable against the mares' opening maiden which was two seconds slower.

Bought expensively as a three-year-old for a €155,000 at the Goffs Land Rover Stores Sale in June 2019 by Colin Bowe's Milestone Bloodstock, connections were rightly disappointed when he only fetched a bid of £135,000 at the Goffs UK Summer Mixed Sale in July and led the gelding out unsold.

Experience will not be lost on this promising sort. He has everything in his make-up to develop into a decent track performer.

REVELS HILL
5YO BAY GELDING

TRAINER:	Harry Fry
PEDIGREE:	Mahler – Chlolo Supreme (Supreme Leader)
FORM (P2P):	U1 -
OPTIMUM TRIP:	2m +
GOING:	Soft

A scopey son of Mahler bought to run in the colours of Noel Fehily's racing syndicate.

Chris Barber's gelding was in the midst of making a promising debut at Milborne St Andrew in early February but unseated at the twelfth fence when still travelling comfortably in second position.

Next seen three weeks later at Badbury Rings, he had clearly learned from his experience and popped out to make all the running under Freddie Procter, surviving one bad blunder at the third from home to return an easy seven-length winner of the incident-packed race.

Out of a half-sister to 2m2f-3m hurdle winner Solomn Grundy and bumper/2m and 2m4f hurdle winner Seamies Dream. His extended family link back to smart hurdle winner Count Campioni.

Revels Hill is an athletic type with scope to jump a fence. He will most likely start in a bumper in the early part of the season before switching to hurdles.

RIPPER ROO
5YO GREY GELDING

TRAINER:	Olly Murphy
PEDIGREE:	Smadoun – Sninfia (Hector Protector)
FORM (P2P):	1 -
OPTIMUM TRIP:	2m +
GOING:	Good to Soft

Ripper Roo is another exciting prospect to graduate from Francesca Nimmo and Charlie Poste's yard.

The good-looking grey made an impressive start to his racing career when coming home the 20-length winner of a 2m 4f maiden at Sheriff Hutton in January – the runner-up has since won easily by nine lengths on his debut over hurdles for Henry De Bromhead.

Partnered with James King, the pair settled well off the early strong pace before making gradual headway after the eighth fence. Keeping tabs on the leaders, the five-year-old jumped safely over the next few fences before moving into second place with three to take. Saving ground up the inside, he moved to the front with the minimal amount of fuss between the final two fences before steadying over the last and scampering right away from Commandingpresence.

Following the race his jockey said, "He came to us 12 months ago from France, he's very professional and better ground along with going right-handed will bring about further improvement in him."

Ripper Roo is a half-brother to a point winner and his dam was a successful 2m-2m4f hurdle/chase winner. The further family link back to a number of Flat performers, including a useful sprinter called Night Flight.

Ripper Roo is certainly one to follow, especially if connections chose to run him in a bumper before tackling hurdles. He has the potential to be very smart.

ROBIN DES SMOKE
5YO BAY MARE

TRAINER:	Richard Phillips
PEDIGREE:	Robin Des Pres – Thanks For Smoking (King's Theatre)
FORM (P2P):	6F731 -
OPTIMUM TRIP:	2m 4f +
GOING:	Soft

Robin Des Smoke is more exposed than most but her good attitude should see her win races.

Benny Walsh's mare showed promise to finish sixth at Dromahane in April 2019 when beaten a little over seven lengths by the subsequent winner Tucanae, before falling two out a month later behind Askdaboss.

Put away for the summer, she finished a detached seventh on her reappearance at Dromahane in November but showed definite signs of improvement a fortnight later when staying on well to clinch third place in a competitive four-year-olds' maiden won by Russellsway at Boulta where she was given a more positive ride.

She found further improvement on a return visit to that track to force a dead-heat with Found On in an 11-runner contest when sent off the 2/1 favourite. Again, ridden prominently, she jumped and travelled well on the heels of the leaders before quickening to the front after the third from home. Readily pulling a few lengths clear of the field, she kept up the gallop and maintained her lead over the next two fences but was joined on the run to the line by John Halley's mare who has since placed in a bumper for Martin Keighley.

Robin Des Smoke boasts only a modest pedigree. Her dam won a point and is a sister to a point/2m1f hurdle winner out of a point/2m4f chase winner.

What sets this mare apart is her unquestionable attitude. She's not the biggest individual but she's hardy and will win her fair share of races, albeit probably at a lower level.

ROBIN DES THEATRE
5YO BAY/BROWN MARE

TRAINER:	Michael Scudamore
PEDIGREE:	Robin Des Champs – Shannon Theatre (King's Theatre)
FORM (P2P):	1 -
OPTIMUM TRIP:	2m 4f +
GOING:	Soft

A likeable mare who should pay her way.

Robin Des Theatre was well backed to make a winning debut in the five-and six-year-old mares' maiden at Tinahely in January and didn't disappoint her followers when obliging comfortably by one and a half lengths from the more experienced Lawlor's Choice who has since gone on to win her own maiden.

Trained by Donnchadh Doyle and ridden by local jockey, James Walsh, the mare enjoyed the front-running tactics and settled into a lovely rhythm over her fences. Still bounding along with ears pricked after the third from home, the field started to close the four-length lead as they hit the rising ground but she responded generously for pressure and kept her advantage approaching the penultimate fence. Comprehensively outjumping her nearest pursuer and gaining a length in the air, she touched down with momentum and battled bravely on the run to the last. Again, meeting the fence in her stride, she got away quickly and galloped on relentlessly all the way to the line.

It is a long way home up the hill from the third last, but this mare, despite being in the van the entire way, relished the test and kept digging into her stamina reserves to fend off the challengers. Her clean jumping was also an asset and enabled her to conserve energy in the soft ground.

The five-year-old is a half-sister to Tom Lacey's 2m5f winner, Colt Lightning. Her full sister, Toodlepip, has shown signs of promise in four starts for Harry Fry.

Her purchase price of £50,000 could underrate her as I'm sure she'll be well capable of winning races. Courses like Chepstow, Ffos Las and Exeter should suit as they would bring her stamina into play.

ROSSBEIGH STRAND
5YO BAY GELDING

TRAINER: Richard Phillips
PEDIGREE: Mahler – Could Do (Cloudings)
FORM (P2P): P/1 -
OPTIMUM TRIP: 2m +
GOING: Soft/Heavy

Rossbeigh Strand looks a nice addition to Adlestrop Stables.

The David Kelly-trained gelding is a late foal, born in June 2015, and possibly needed more time when pulling up on his debut at Dromahane in April 2019 – a race won by one of last year's pointing graduates, Bobhopeornohope.

Put away for the rest of the season, he reappeared in January of this year at Aghabullogue and was given a positive, no-nonsense ride by James Hannon who booted him to the front when the flags went up. Appearing to relish the testing conditions, the five-year-old rose to the task and produced a polished round of jumping and readily came clear of the field after the penultimate fence (usually three from home) to win by 14 lengths, despite a bad blunder at the last – his only mistake of the race.

On the eye, this was an impressive performance and the form has held up OK with the third a winner next time. The distance of ground he opened up, despite the soft/heavy conditions, was indicative of a classy performance and it suitable impressed Gerry Hogan who purchased the gelding from the Goffs Doncaster Sale in January for £38,000.

Out of a 3m hurdle winner who is a half-sister to a 2m hurdle winner from the family of Stayers' Hurdle winner Anzum.

I'm sure Richard Phillips, who places his horses to such great effect, will find plenty of winning opportunities for Rossbeigh Strand.

SHIROCCO'S DREAM
5YO BAY MARE

TRAINER:	Colin Tizzard
PEDIGREE:	Shirocco – Dream Function (King's Theatre)
FORM (P2P):	21 -
OPTIMUM TRIP:	2m +
GOING:	Soft

☆ **STAR POTENTIAL** ☆

Shirocco's Dream looks an exciting mare with some smart form.

The Donnchadh Doyle-trained five-year-old ran a race full of promise to finish second to Rose Of Arcadia on her debut at Tattersalls Farm in December 2019. It was a race where the winner got away from the field and although this mare did well to bridge the deficit, the line came just in time for the winner who prevailed by two lengths. Rose Of Arcadia was subsequently purchased by Colin Tizzard and franked the form by winning under Rules at the first time of asking.

Shirocco's Dream was given a short break and returned to action at Borris House in March and was unsurprisingly sent off the evens favourite under Rob James. Sitting in second place for the majority of the three miles, she moved up to challenge the long-time leader at the third from home and produced a good leap which took her into a narrow advantage.

Challenged by a new rival over the penultimate fence, the mare lost her lead but battled gamely on the approach to the last and produced a much-needed spring-heeled leap before pulling out all the stops on the run to the line. Showing a resilient attitude and a change of gear, she overhauled the leader to win by half a length with a further 18 lengths back to the third.

This was a smart performance by the mare and she has since been snapped up by Colin Tizzard for £260,000 at the Cheltenham Festival Sale in March.

A half-sister to bumper winner Arion Sky, her dam is a full sister to the 169-rated Grade 1 winner Captain Chris.

Already highlighting herself as an exciting individual to follow, she should certainly have plenty to offer her new connections.

Shirocco's Dream displaying tremendous courage en route to victory (Picture by Emma O'Brien)

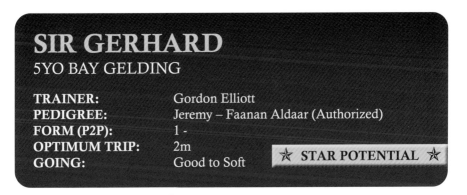

SIR GERHARD
5YO BAY GELDING

TRAINER:	Gordon Elliott
PEDIGREE:	Jeremy – Faanan Aldaar (Authorized)
FORM (P2P):	1 -
OPTIMUM TRIP:	2m
GOING:	Good to Soft

☆ **STAR POTENTIAL** ☆

Gordon Elliott looks to have another top prospect on his hands.

The Ellmarie Holden-trained bay made light work of the opposition on his debut in a four-year-old geldings' maiden at Boulta in November 2019, coming home a very easy 12-length winner from Minella Drama who went on to finish a close second on his next start.

The fourth also highlighted the form by winning on his next outing, and The Bees Knees who fell at the last when weakening out of contention added further strength to the contest when scoring next time and has since finished third in a bumper for Fergal O'Brien.

Sir Gerhard moved with purpose at the head of affairs and settled into a lovely jumping rhythm, measuring his fences accurately and wasting no time in the air. Still full of running after taking the fourth from home, Derek O'Connor stole a look over his shoulder and quickened the tempo before the next. Slightly outjumped by The Bees Knees, Sir Gerhard's superior speed immediately recouped the lost ground and he pressed on around the home bend.

With ears pricked approaching the penultimate fence, he popped over nicely and was soon clear on the run to the last. One final perfect leap sealed the race and he coasted up the run-in to record a wide-margin success.

Purchased as a three-year-old at the Goffs Land Rover Sale for €72,000, he certainly surpassed that expensive price tag when selling to Gordon Elliott for £400,000 at Cheltenham's December Sale.

The five-year-old is the first foal out of Faanan Aldaar, a 2m hurdle winner who was also placed on the Flat over 1m2f-1m4f. She is a half-sister to an all-weather Listed winner over 7f and the further family extend back to the 1m Group 1 winner Zafeen.

With such a bias towards speed in his pedigree, I fully expect Sir Gerhard to have the requisite pace for bumpers. Could he provide Cheveley Park with their third successive Cheltenham Festival Champion Bumper?

Could Sir Gerhard make it three in a row for Cheveley Park in the Cheltenham Festival Champion Bumper? (Picture by Tattersalls)

SIR SHOLOKHOV
5YO BAY GELDING

TRAINER:	Harry Whittington
PEDIGREE:	Sholokhov – Menepresents (Presenting)
FORM (P2P):	1 -
OPTIMUM TRIP:	2m +
GOING:	Good to Soft

Sir Sholokhov's gutsy attitude will hold him in good stead under Rules.

The Michael Goff-trained five-year-old was one of only a handful of newcomers to feature in the 12-strong line-up for the third division of the four-year-olds' maiden at Mainstown in December and was sent off at odds of 3/1 under Shane Fitzgerald.

Given a patient ride in the soft ground, the gelding was positioned towards the rear for the main part of the race before making gradual headway through horses on the run to the fourth from home. After a good jump he quickly latched on to the heels of the leaders and continued to move well before being nudged along for a stride after clearing the third last.

Scrubbed along in fourth position rounding the bend for home, victory looked unlikely, but the gelding kept finding for pressure and produced a good leap over the penultimate fence before switching to the inside for a clearer passage. Still over a length down on the leader approaching the last, he continued to battle and came up well over the fence before responding gamely on the run-in to get up in the dying strides and beat the more experienced Here We Have It by a head.

This looked like a good race and although the form is yet to be franked, the time was quick and the runner-up has since gone on to fill the frame twice more.

Sir Sholokhov is a half-brother to On The Short List, a winner of a good point-to-point in 2018 but hasn't been seen since. His dam, by Presenting, placed in a bumper and over hurdles and is a sister to a 2m1f hurdle winner.

It's likely that, despite winning on soft ground, the bay will be better suited to sounder underfoot conditions. He could show up well in a bumper, but I expect him to come into his own over a longer trip.

The intelligent-looking Sir Sholokhov waiting to be sold (Picture by Tattersalls)

STAR GATE
4YO BAY GELDING

TRAINER:	Evan Williams
PEDIGREE:	Imperial Monarch – Supreme Judge (Brian Boru)
FORM (P2P):	1 -
OPTIMUM TRIP:	2m 4f +
GOING:	Good to Soft

Evan Williams could have a lovely type on his hands with this close relation to Amberleigh House.

Star Gate made his debut in a competitive four-year-olds' maiden at Bellharbour in February – a race which was left open with the departure of the 6/4 joint-favourite Petibonome at the fifth from home.

Never too far from the pace, the racy son of Imperial Monarch produced a polished round of jumping and challenged for the lead with a quick leap over the third from home. Slightly slower at the next, Rob James nudged him along for a stride or two which was met with an immediate response as he quickly moved back to the front as they swung off the turn for home. Despite a tendency to hang to his left, he produced an impressive turn of foot on the run to the last and readily opened up a healthy advantage before keeping on well to the line to beat the strongly fancied Womalko by three lengths.

Visually, this was a very taking performance from Star Gate and although the clock didn't record a favourable time due to the sedate pace, the potent turn of foot the gelding produced on the run to the last will be a deadly weapon when racing under Rules.

Purchased for £140,000 at the Cheltenham Sale in February.

Star Gate should have the requisite pace for bumpers but there's stamina on both sides of his pedigree and I fully expect him to need a trip as he matures.

STREET VALUE
5YO BAY GELDING

TRAINER:	TBC
PEDIGREE:	Well Chosen – Carrigbuck (Buckskin)
FORM (P2P):	2 -
OPTIMUM TRIP:	2m 4f +
GOING:	Soft

Street Value showed plenty of potential on his debut.

John Flavin's son of Well Chosen was one of only two newcomers to line up in the eight-runner field for the five-year-old geldings' maiden at Ballyarthur in March.

Ridden positively by James Hannon, the gelding travelled with a spring in his step and bounded to four from home with a slender advantage before being challenged on the run to the next. Gamely responding to keep his nose in front, he jumped safely but got in tight to the penultimate fence and dropped back to third.

Ridden along but tenacious in response when forced three wide, he moved back alongside the two leaders turning out of the back straight before moving into a clear second as they climbed the hill for home. Rallying again as they bypassed the final fence, the bay closed the gap with the eventual winner who was benefiting from three previous starts.

This was a courageous debut from Street Value and although the form has had no time to be franked, the time was in line with the other races run on the card.

Closely related to the useful 2m-3m7f hurdle/chase winner Cloudy Morning and point winner Silver Serenade. His dam is an unraced sister to the useful 2m2f-2m6f hurdle/chase winner Yellow Spring.

Street Value was withdrawn from the sales in July but has highlighted himself as a thoroughly genuine sort to watch out for.

STRIKING A POSE
4YO BAY GELDING

TRAINER:	Colin Tizzard
PEDIGREE:	Getaway – Clonsingle Native (Be My Native)
FORM (P2P):	1 -
OPTIMUM TRIP:	2m 4f +
GOING:	Soft

Colin Tizzard knows this family well as he trains the full brother Nativegetaway.

Striking A Pose is a tall, leggy individual and it is testament to his natural ability that he was able to show so much on his British pointing debut at Brocklesby Park in mid-February where he sauntered clear up the run-in to win by 25 lengths.

Six runners went to post for the 3m contest which was run in a heavy downpour and altered the going from good to soft, to soft. Undeterred by the conditions, the son of Getaway looked comfortable on the ground and was never too far off the pace throughout. Moving up to challenge at the second from home the gelding quickly asserted and, despite a slow leap at the last, he drew clear up the run-in with Gina Andrews punching the air in delight as she crossed the line.

After the race Tom Ellis said, "He's a classy sort with a very good pedigree and one of our better four-year-olds in the yard."

Sent to the Cheltenham February Sale six days later, he was purchased by Ross Doyle, acting on behalf of Colin Tizzard. Colin's son, Joe, said, "We thought he was the best-looking horse here. He looked really well for a horse who had run last weekend."

Striking A Pose, as mentioned, is a full brother to his now stable companion Nativegetaway. He is also a half-brother to bumper/2m3f-3m1f hurdle/smart chaser Ackertac, who was trained by Nigel Twiston-Davies.

The bay is likely to need time to come to hand and will no doubt be brought along steadily. I would expect him to need 2m 4f over hurdles sooner rather than later.

SUPREME JET
4YO BAY GELDING

TRAINER:	TBC
PEDIGREE:	Jet Away – Pollys Leader (Supreme Leader)
FORM (P2P):	1 -
OPTIMUM TRIP:	2m +
GOING:	Good to Soft

Supreme Jet could not have been more impressive in winning the same 2m 4f Oldtown maiden which produced subsequent Grade 1 winner Asterion Forlonge.

The Jet Away gelding went to the front from the drop of the flag and quickly established a considerable lead by the time he had reached the third fence. Allowed a breather at the halfway point, his advantage halved but with some slick jumping over the fifth and fourth from home, he pressed on again and rounded the home turn 15 lengths clear of the field.

Still travelling powerfully, he produced another spring-heeled leap over the third from home and his jockey, Pa King, took a look over both shoulders before letting out an inch of rein. The field began to close on the downhill run to the penultimate fence and closed to within five lengths, but Supreme Jet kept up the gallop and despite being understandably tired when making a mistake over the last, he kept on determinedly all the way to the line to win by three and a half lengths.

Following the race, trainer Patrick Farrell said, "We knew he was special before Christmas. We ran him down in Tipperary in a schooling bumper and he finished beside Apple's Jade. From then on, we were just taking our time with him and getting him ready".

Surprisingly, he was led out of the ring unsold for £95,000 at Cheltenham in February and it's yet to be seen where he'll end up.

From a well-bred family of winners, which includes the seven-time track winners Gatflax and In The Blood.

Supreme Jet obviously has plenty of ability and looks set for a successful campaign under Rules.

TAG MAN
4YO BAY GELDING

TRAINER:	TBC
PEDIGREE:	Fame And Glory – Annie Spectrim (Spectrum)
FORM (P2P):	2 -
OPTIMUM TRIP:	2m 4f +
GOING:	Soft

Tag Man showed a game attitude in defeat on his debut at Borris House in March and looks a potential improver.

The Mary Doyle-trained newcomer was given a patient ride by John O'Neill before making notable progress to close on the pacesetters at the halfway point. Sitting in a share of third place approaching the fourth from home, the gelding was a little slow to take off which caused him to lose his position and need assistance from the saddle upon touching down. Quickly recovering his position before the next, he produced a better leap to take him on to the heels of the leader, Amarillo Sky, and the pair pressed on rounding the turn for home.

Asked for an effort on the approach to the penultimate fence, the bay responded generously to move alongside and almost touch down with the lead before battling valiantly on the run to the last. Despite giving everything and jumping the fence well, the winner was too strong in the finish and went on to win by three parts of a length with a further 15 lengths back to the third.

Tag Man did very little wrong in defeat and was beaten by a smart-looking individual who has subsequently been purchased at the Cheltenham Festival Sale to join Colin Tizzard's yard for £280,000. Tag Man was sold at the same sale for £135,000 and will now run in the colours of Roger Brookhouse.

Out of an unraced half-sister to Sonevafushi, a useful 2m-3m3f hurdle/chase winner, and Celtic Son, a bumper/useful 2m5f-3m1f hurdle/chase winner. His half-brother, It's All About Me, was successful over hurdles (2m7f).

By Fame And Glory out of a Spectrum mare, I expect Tag Man to have some pace, but judging by his family and the way he moved through his race, he looked like a stayer who would appreciate softer ground.

TALLOW FOR COAL
4YO BAY GELDING

TRAINER:	Jamie Snowden
PEDIGREE:	Arctic Cosmos – South Queen Lady (King's Ride)
FORM (P2P):	1 -
OPTIMUM TRIP:	2m 4f +
GOING:	Soft

Tallow For Coal was able to come home as he liked to win the same 2m 4f Knockanard maiden that Ferny Hollow emerged victorious from 12 months ago.

Weather conditions were not ideal, and the fixture was eventually abandoned after the third race, but that didn't stop this four-year-old by Arctic Cosmos who displayed plenty of natural pace to help force the early fractions and eventually assert his advantage going out on to the final circuit.

Pulling four lengths clear of the field after taking the fourth from home, he survived a terrible blunder at the third last – a fence which claimed his two nearest pursuers – but was afforded time to recover before taking the final two fences in his own time to eventually cross the line a distance clear of the only other finisher.

Following the race his handler said, "He's a horse that does everything right; he wouldn't be an outstanding work horse but the best racehorses aren't always the best work horses! … he was hardy enough to break, but he's very relaxed now. Once he got the hang of it then, he was grand. He's a very straightforward horse that does everything that you ask him to do."

Despite showing speed, Tallow For Coal is by Arctic Cosmos out of a King's Ride mare which indicates he will be seen to best effect when the emphasis is on stamina. His half-sisters include Humbie and Fille Des Champs who were both successful over three miles. His dam was placed in a point-to-point and is out of a sister to the useful staying chaser Occold and half-sister to Polly Puttens (dam of Denman).

Bought for £50,000 by Tom Malone on behalf of Jamie Snowden at Cheltenham's February Sale.

Jamie Snowden's Tallow For Coal could be a good purchase for £50,000 (Picture by Tattersalls)

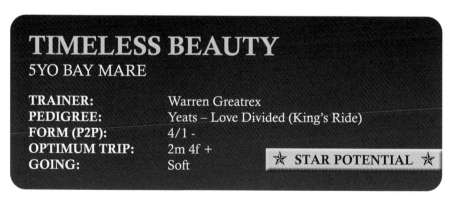

TIMELESS BEAUTY
5YO BAY MARE

TRAINER:	Warren Greatrex
PEDIGREE:	Yeats – Love Divided (King's Ride)
FORM (P2P):	4/1 -
OPTIMUM TRIP:	2m 4f +
GOING:	Soft

★ **STAR POTENTIAL** ★

The McNeill Family should have plenty of fun with this mare.

The daughter of Yeats showed plenty of promise to finish fourth at Inch on her debut in April 2019 but made a few minor jumping errors late in the race and didn't quite have the pace to get on terms with the leaders.

Perhaps needing time to develop physically, she was put away for the summer and returned to action at Oldtown in February 2020 where she was heavily supported and sent off the 4/6 favourite under Jamie Scallan.

Always prominent, Timeless Beauty travelled strongly in the testing conditions and took closer order with a good leap over the third from home. Continuing to sit on the heels of the leaders on the downhill run, she then touched down with a narrow advantage over the penultimate fence. Ridden along to assert, she responded generously and pulled clear on the run to the last where she produced a big leap before galloping on relentlessly to the line to win by a comfortable three lengths.

This was a strong performance from the mare who still had plenty more to give. The patient handling from her trainer which allowed her time to grow and develop certainly paid off and should stand her in good stead for the future.

Sent to the Cheltenham Sales six days after her victory, she sold the way of the McNeill Family for £100,000 and will now join Warren Greatrex's yard.

I have a fondness for mares by Yeats. They always seem to give everything in their races and have tremendous attitudes. We will see the best of this one when the ground is soft and she tackles trips in excess of 2m 4f.

UPANDATIT
5YO BAY GELDING

TRAINER:	Nick Alexander
PEDIGREE:	Winged Love – Betty Beck (Westerner)
FORM (P2P):	33 -
OPTIMUM TRIP:	2m 4f +
GOING:	Soft

☆ **STAR POTENTIAL** ☆

Upandatit looks sure to pay his way for his northern-based handler.

The Warren Ewing-trained son of Winged Love made his debut in a very competitive four-year-olds' maiden at Loughanmore in October 2019 where he stayed on eye-catchingly from the rear over the final couple of fences to chase home Fiston Des Issards – subsequently purchased for £255,000 – and Boothill who bolted up in a bumper at Kempton for Harry Fry. A head behind Upandatit in fourth was Smurphy Enki who boosted the form further when winning by 18 lengths on his debut for Chris Gordon.

Upandatit posted another promising effort when filling the same position on his final start between the flags at Mainstown in December. Ridden more prominently on this occasion, the gelding moved well throughout and was almost alongside the leader approaching the fourth from home but was slow through the air and touched down in third place.

Holding that position over the next, he was hard ridden around the home bend but responded willingly to fend off a whole host of challengers before slightly overjumping at the penultimate fence causing him to peck on landing. Quickly gathered up, the bay stuck to his task well and produced a spring-heeled leap over the last before chasing home Junior Rattler and Across The Channel, who scored by a neck with a further three lengths to Upandatit.

A half-brother to 2m2f hurdle winner Paddy Buns, his dam is an unraced half-sister to bumper winner Nana Joan out of the 2m/2m3f hurdle winning half-sister to Velka Pardubicka winner Registana.

Purchased privately, this stoutly bred gelding has joined Nick Alexander. He has shown more than enough to suggest he can win over hurdles. Trips which bring his stamina into play are likely to suit best.

WESTERN ZARA
4YO GREY FILLY

TRAINER:	Paul Nolan
PEDIGREE:	Westerner – Flemerelle (Flemensfirth)
FORM (P2P):	2 -
OPTIMUM TRIP:	2m 4f +
GOING:	Soft

Western Zara made an encouraging start to her career and looks capable of track success.

The Johnny Berry-trained grey finished second to the useful Chosen Port on her debut at Ballycahane in March, just six days prior to being sold to Gerry Hogan at the Cheltenham Festival Sale for £85,000.

Always towards the fore, the daughter of Westerner travelled smoothly within her comfort zone and picked up the running with four fences left to jump. Bounding along with ears pricked, she jumped the next couple of fences nicely and continued to hold her advantage on the downhill run to two out. Again, she was nimble and got away quickly before turning into the straight where she upped the tempo. Hanging slightly under pressure on the long run to the last, she was challenged and passed by the eventual winner but battled bravely, jumping the last well before sticking on tenaciously in the closing stages to close to within two lengths.

This was a nice performance by the four-year-old who showed herself to have a very game attitude to rally after the last having led a long way from home. She's only a petite model but she's athletic and will probably be seen in a greater light in a race with a stronger pace.

Western Zara is a first foal out of a half-sister to Boberelle (bumper winner) and Special Bar (2m3f hurdle winner), with the further family linking back to the smart 2m hurdler Winter Squall and impressive five-time hurdle winner (including Grade 2) Carobee.

There's plenty to like about Western Zara. She may have enough speed to win a bumper but I expect her to flourish in handicaps once stepped up in trip to 2m 4f or even three miles.

Western Zara could prove a smart filly for Paul Nolan (Picture by Tattersalls)

WILD ROMANCE
5YO BROWN MARE

TRAINER:	Dan Skelton
PEDIGREE:	Kalanisi – Aboo Lala (Aboo Hom)
FORM (P2P):	2 -
OPTIMUM TRIP:	2m 4f +
GOING:	Good to Soft

Wild Romance looks a likely improver.

The Denis Murphy-trained mare fared best of the seven newcomers when finishing second on her debut in a 17-runner four-year-olds' maiden at Boulta in November 2019.

Always in rear, she needed plenty of encouragement to pick up the bridle but stayed on takingly in the latter stages and arrived on to the scene with half a chance jumping the penultimate fence. Continuing to stay on, she moved into second approaching the last but was unable to sustain her effort up the run-in and was beaten by two and a half lengths.

This was an eye-catching performance from the mare who is entitled to come on considerably for her first racecourse experience.

A half-sister to 2m3f chase winner Inch Lala, point winner Maliboo and also 2m4f-3m hurdle winner Boss Man Fred who is also trained by Dan Skelton. His dam was a point winner and a sister to a 2m4f hunter chaser.

Wild Romance doesn't look the biggest – typical of Kalanisi's offspring – but she does have plenty of stamina and could come into her own in long-distance handicap hurdles this term.

WILL CARVER
5YO BAY GELDING

TRAINER:	Nicky Henderson
PEDIGREE:	Califet – Rock Angel (Desert King)
FORM (P2P):	F41 -
OPTIMUM TRIP:	2m
GOING:	Good to Soft

This good-looking five-year-old is set to carry the colours of Owners Group having been purchased for £60,000 by Highflyer Bloodstock.

Will Carver fell when looking held at the third from home on his debut at Borris House in December but fared much better when filling fourth position at Dromahane later in the month. That was quite a competitive 14-runner maiden but the gelding travelled and jumped well just off the pace and was still in with a chance until only finding the one pace when the leaders quickened on the long run to the penultimate fence.

Putting that experience to good use, the bay got off the mark at the third time of asking when making all to win a seven-runner maiden at Kirkistown in February. Perhaps appreciating the slightly better ground conditions, he skipped along at the front and produced a bold round of jumping before showing a bright turn of foot as the race developed into a sprint on the long run for home where the final fence was omitted.

The time recorded was slow in comparison to the other races on the card but Will Carver showed himself to have a useful turn of foot which bodes well if he were to contest a bumper in his first season under Rules.

Will Carver is a half-brother to Henry De Bromhead's useful 2m Grade 2 winner Jason The Militant. His dam was also successful over two miles as a hurdler and is a sister to bumper/1m4f-1m6f/2m hurdle winner Kinger Rocks out of a useful 1m2f-1m4f winner.

Everything about this gelding suggests he should pay his way when the emphasis is on speed. Better ground may also be the key to his useful turn of foot.

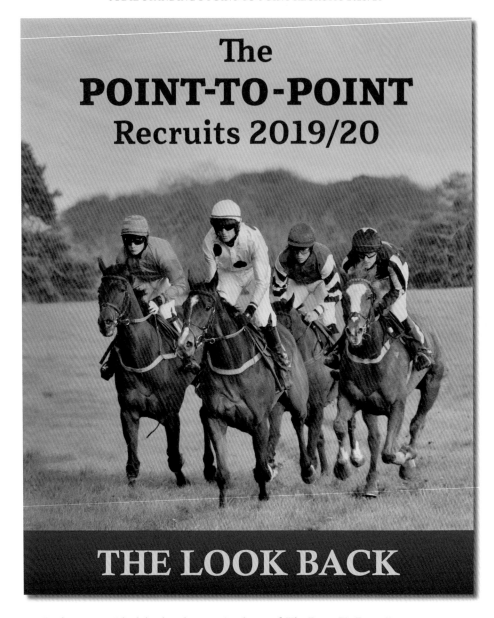

The POINT-TO-POINT Recruits 2019/20

THE LOOK BACK

In this section I look back at last year's edition of The Point-To-Point Recruits. We enjoyed some fantastic results but other recruits will take longer to fulfil their promise.

After such a successful first edition of *The Point-To-Point Recruits*, the tricky part was always going to be following up the year after but, thankfully, I am more than pleased to say I think we did just that with the 2019/20 edition.

I have a few favourites from last year's book, but I think the right place to start is with the Cheltenham Festival Champion Bumper winner, **Ferny Hollow**.

Willie Mullins' £300,000 purchase was odds-on to make a winning debut at Fairyhouse back in December, but the Westerner gelding was a tricky ride for Patrick Mullins and could only finish second. It was a similar story later that month at Leopardstown's Christmas meeting where he found Forged In Fire a half-length too good for him.

Ferny Hollow

Fitted with a hood and ridden more patiently on his return to Fairyhouse in late February – a final chance saloon to book his ticket for the boat to the Festival – the penny finally dropped for the five-year-old and he produced a performance his supporters had been expecting from the start.

Partnered by Paul Townend for the Grade 1 Champion Bumper at the Cheltenham Festival due to Patrick Mullins electing to ride the favourite, Appreciate It, Ferny Hollow was given an inspired ride by the County Cork jockey and came from last to first, showing a useful turn of foot before staying on strongly to beat his stable companion by two and a half lengths.

By Westerner out of a Good Thyne mare, Ferny Hollow will most likely develop into a horse who will appreciate a test of stamina as he gets older. However, for the time being he possesses the required speed to make a serious impact in the 2m hurdle division with the Supreme Novices' Hurdle likely to be his main target.

Ruth Jefferson has been a lucky trainer for me, with Mega Yeats providing my first success as an author in the 2018/19 edition of *The Point-To-Point Recruits.*

Last year, **Clondaw Caitlin**, although unsuccessful in three attempts in points, proved a star performer by winning four times on the bounce under Rules, including a bumper at Wetherby followed by an eight-length beating of Rayna's World when upped in trip to an extended 2m 3f on her first attempt over hurdles on a return to the Yorkshire track. She then thrashed Sophie Fatale by 10 lengths at Newcastle under a penalty and latterly beat the geldings in a Grade 2 at Kelso by five lengths in February.

Clondaw Caitlin

Clondaw Caitlin is an imposing mare with a thoroughly likeable attitude. She will be sent novice chasing this term and I dare say she'll improve for the fences.

Ruth also trained **Blossoming Forth** – a mare I had high hopes for and one I nominated as having 'star potential'.

Unlike her stable companion, the Flemensfirth mare had winning form in a point but she failed to replicate that on five occasions under Rules. She raced awkwardly on her last two starts, which could have been a sign of immaturity or maybe she was feeling something. Whatever the case, if her trainer can get to the bottom of her troubles, she may prove to be well treated on her mark of 105. She may even go for a novices' handicap chase.

David Pipe, another trainer who has provided me with plenty of success, carried on the tradition with **Make Me A Believer** and Israel Champ.

The former was a gutsy all-the-way winner of a bumper at Chepstow's opening meeting in October, with some punters availing themselves of the early overnight odds of 20/1. The five-year-old hasn't been seen since, but did hold an entry up until the declaration stage for the Champion Bumper at Cheltenham, suggesting he was still in training in spring.

Israel Champ quickly left a disappointing debut at Worcester behind him by defying odds of 16/1 to win the Listed bumper at Cheltenham's BetVictor meeting in November before carrying his penalty to success in another Listed contest at Ascot the following month – a race connections won the previous year with Eden Du Houx.

The five-year-old was well beaten in the Champion Bumper at Cheltenham on his final start but remains an exciting novice hurdles prospect this season. He's a very strong individual – built for fences – and we are yet to see the best of him.

Another multiple winner – and the first winner from last year's publication – was Nigel Twiston-Davies' **Mossy Fen**.

I never expected this stout-staying son of Milan to show as much in his first season under Rules but it's testament to his natural ability, his underlying class and his connections' excellent placing which saw him win three times, including a tremendously game effort to capture the Grade 2 Leamington Novices'

Mossy Fen

Hurdle at Warwick when given a brilliant ride by Sam Twiston-Davies.

He signed off his season with a thoroughly respectable effort to finish fifth – beaten 23 lengths – behind Envoi Allen in the Ballymore Novices' Hurdle at the Cheltenham Festival and is now set to go novice chasing.

With a physique which suggests he will relish the switch to fences, he's certainly one to be excited about.

Another recruit with the potential to develop into a smart novice chaser is **Sporting John**.

Philip Hobbs' son of Getaway impressed me when winning a point-to-point at Borris House and he quickly established himself as a leading novice hurdler. On his debut at Exeter over 2m 1f he beat the subsequent Grade 2 winner Harry Senior by a little under two lengths and later defied his penalty over the same course and distance, drawing clear inside the final two furlongs to win by an easy eight lengths from Buckhorn George.

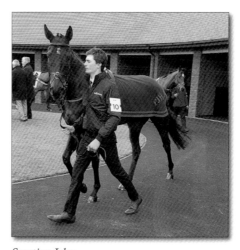

Sporting John

Given a two-month break, he returned to land the hat-trick at Ascot in February where he was stepped up in trip to 2m 3½f for a tightly knit four-runner novices' hurdle. Again, he stayed on strongly in the closing stages, relishing the extra distance.

Sent to the Cheltenham Festival for an eagerly awaited clash with Envoi Allen in the Ballymore Novices' Hurdle, the five-year-old never looked at ease or travelled with his usual enthusiasm and returned a distant seventh. Following the disappointment, he was reported as finishing stressed, and his trainer later said he appeared 'odd behind' but pulled out fine the next morning.

Set to go chasing this season, he has the ability to progress into a serious candidate for something like the JLT Novices' Chase come March.

Hobbs also trains **Truckers Pass** who finished second in a couple of bumpers. Firstly he bumped into Soaring Glory on his debut where he was pipped in the final strides, and then he found Tile Tapper just under two lengths too good for him at Exeter on New Year's Day.

A scopey, classy sort, we haven't even begun to scratch the surface with him yet and he remains with the potential to be a high-class sort.

The Big Breakaway was another who lined up in this year's Ballymore Novices' Hurdle. He stayed on well to finish a creditable fourth, just over fourteen lengths behind the winner.

Colin Tizzard is no stranger to buying youngsters with the future very much in the forefront of his mind, and this scopey chestnut looks the perfect type to flourish once he sees a fence.

The Big Breakaway

Unbeaten over hurdles going into the Festival having won impressively on his debut at Chepstow in November followed by a seven-length beating of Papa Tango Charly at Newbury in December. A step up to three miles should suit the strong stayer, with the RSA the ultimate aim at the end of the season.

Tizzard also trains **Royal Crown** who remains a maiden after three starts over hurdles. The handicapper has given him a mark of 108, which could be within reach when he encounters some nicer ground than the soft and heavy he raced on last winter.

Fergal O'Brien moved to his new yard – Ravenswell Farm – last season and the winners have been flooding in ever since.

It's never easy for a horse to defy a penalty in a bumper, never mind a double penalty, but that's exactly what **Ask A Honey Bee** did at Wetherby under an enterprising ride from the front by young Liam Harrison in February. The pair had already teamed up to win by 11 lengths at Haydock in late December, following on from the horse's game debut victory under Paddy Brennan at Southwell the previous month.

Ask A Honey Bee

The six-year-old displayed both courage and a willing attitude in four point-to-points prior to racing under Rules and that wealth of experience will not be lost on him as he embarks on his career over hurdles.

Brief Ambition also experienced success at the first time of asking when getting up in the shadows of the post to beat the sadly ill-fated Supamouse at Southwell in October. He went on to finish fourth to Israel Champ in the Listed bumper at Cheltenham in November before filling the runner-up spot in another Listed event at Newbury on Betfair Hurdle day behind Ocean Wind, finding only the one pace. Beaten a long way in the Champion Bumper, he looks ready for a step up in trip when he embarks on his career over hurdles.

The third horse I featured from Fergal's yard was **Minella Tara**, also a winner at the first time of asking under Rules. That was on the all-weather in a bumper around Lingfield, but he failed to follow up in a stronger contest at Kempton in February. He's better than he showed that day and is another who should be placed effectively over timber.

Another multiple winner was Tom Lacey's **Adrimel**.

This son of Tirwanako never saw a rival when making all to win by 26 lengths on his debut at Uttoxeter and followed up under a penalty in a stronger race at Doncaster, beating the well-regarded The Edgar Wallace (subsequently won at Hereford) by a little over a length in a good tussle to the line.

Unable to land a blow in the Cheltenham Festival Champion Bumper, he was up with the pace for a long way but gradually weakened when ridden inside the final furlong, crossing the line 40 lengths behind the winner.

I have to say, despite the strong 23-runner line-up, he definitely stood out as one of the picks of the paddock. He's a strong, classy sort who walked around with real presence and swagger. I am looking forward to his season over hurdles. He remains a very exciting individual.

Paul Nicholls' **Cill Anna** was kept busy last season and relished the switch to hurdles having failed to trouble the judge in a couple of bumpers, including a Listed contest around Cheltenham. Following the application of a tongue-tie, she went on to win three times culminating in a Listed hurdle success at Doncaster at the end of February. She's still only five, but I imagine her trainer will want to crack on with her chasing campaign where she can continue to pay her way.

Bravemansgame should show us plenty more this season. The imposing five-year-old was never going to be suited to bumpers but he showed glimpses of his potential when staying on eye-catchingly into third behind Soaring Glory at Ascot on his debut and later finished sixth to Israel Champ. I expect we'll see him take a big step forward when he makes his debut over hurdles.

Jeremy Pass, **Barbados Buck's**, **Skatman**, **Switch Hitter** and **Young Buck** were also lightly raced by the Ditcheat trainer last term and should be found winning opportunities. The latter showed good potential on his one try over hurdles.

Jonjo O'Neill will be hoping **Papa Tango Charly** can get his act together this season.

The expensive £440,000 2019 Aintree Sales purchase stayed on steadily into seventh on his bumper debut at Worcester in October, and although he built on that when finishing second on his hurdling debut at Ascot over 2m 3½f the following month, he was no match for The Big Breakaway at

Newbury over a furlong further and then disappointed at Doncaster in the new year when beaten 34 lengths into fourth by Glynn.

Admittedly, as the old cliché goes, anything he did over hurdles would be a bonus, and I imagine he will thrive over larger obstacles. Quite a raw and weak-looking sort last season, the time away from the track will have done him the world of good and he should be followed closely if he contests a novices' handicap chase from a mark of 128.

Pens Man should also have more to offer from his lowly rating of 102. The strongly built Sholokhov gelding shaped with hints of promise despite finishing down the field in a few maiden/novice hurdle races last season and stuck on well when stepped up in trip on his handicap and seasonal debut at Fontwell in August.

Similarly, **Meyer Lansky** (finished third behind Papa Tango Charly in his point-to-point) should find opportunities, perhaps over fences, to win from his mark of 114. Soft ground and three miles may be the key to him.

Big Bresil who finished second – splitting Meyer Lansky and Papa Tango Charly – on his sole pointing venture shaped encouragingly on his bumper debut at Exeter, plugging on steadily behind Red Rookie, despite being one of the first off the bridle, to fill the runner-up spot in January.

He then returned to Exeter the following month for his hurdling bow and relished the step up in trip to 2m 2½f to beat Lamanver Storm, staying on determinedly from the back of the last to win by a length.

Big Bresil is a big chasing type with bags of stamina. With only two starts under Rules, and only one over hurdles, he may stay over the smaller obstacles for another season, although I fully expect him to thrive when he sees a fence. He has the potential and the ability to go a long way.

Escaria Ten also has the potential to take his form up a notch when encountering fences. Of all the recruits in last year's book, this gelding is chief amongst my favourites.

The six-year-old wasted no time in bumpers after finishing second on his Rules debut in October and was quickly switched to hurdles and upped in trip to 2m 4f at Fairyhouse the following month where he shaped with eye-catching encouragement under a considerate ride from Davy Russell to finish third to Diol Ker (Monkfish finished second).

Bought by the McNeill Family in December, he then won a Cork maiden hurdle over three miles in gutsy fashion before defying his penalty at Ayr over a fraction further, staying on strongly to the line to comfortably beat Portstorm by two and a half lengths.

Sent to Cheltenham to contest the Martin Pipe Conditional Jockeys' Handicap Hurdle from a mark of 136, I strongly fancied his chances, but he never looked relaxed in the rough race and didn't find a whole lot off the bridle when turning into the straight.

Built in the mould of a chaser, I cannot wait for him to tackle the larger obstacles. He will take some beating in a novices' handicap chase from his mark of 132. The softer the ground, the better.

I am looking forward to seeing **Picanha** go hurdling this season.

The six-year-old won his only start in a bumper around Exeter last December – becoming the trainer's first bumper winner in the last five seasons. The Malinas gelding took time to strengthen and reach the racecourse but he can be expected to thrive after another summer on his back.

He'll relish a step up in trip and is a hugely exciting individual for seasons to come.

Donald McCain has a lovely team of young horses to look forward to and chief amongst them is the Tim Leslie-owned **Minella Trump**.

Twice a winner at Sedgefield in novice company (2m 1f and 2m 4f), he then finished second in his first handicap over an extended 2m 3f at Catterick from a mark of 123 before stepping back into novice company over 2m 7f at Bangor where he was first past the post ahead of the 147-rated The Cashel Man, only to lose the race in the stewards' room. He then rounded his season off with a below-par fourth of seven at Newcastle from a mark of 130.

Now six years old, he will most likely head over fences where I believe he will find further improvement. He's a strong stayer with a liking for the mud. He has a lot to offer.

Stable companion **Heartbreak Kid** – also owned by Tim Leslie – hasn't fulfilled the potential he showed when winning his point by 30 lengths at Kirkistown in March 2019. The Getaway gelding was soundly beaten in a couple of maiden hurdles at Bangor and Kelso before coming home alone at Sedgefield where his only rival fell when looking the likely winner.

He's a smooth traveller and a sound jumper but isn't the strongest in a finish. I'm sure he'll turn a corner once the handicapper has assessed him.

Olly Murphy is another trainer with a yard full of talent and **Linelee King** is the one I'm most looking forward to.

We were never going to see the best of the grey in bumpers last year but he managed to win a weak contest at Sedgefield having finished second on his debut at Chepstow. No match for the line-up in the Champion Bumper at Cheltenham, he should have no problem getting off the mark again as a hurdler once stepped up in trip.

Linelee King

He showed a really likeable attitude in his point-to-point and I am hoping that will shine through this season. We won't see the best of him until he sees a fence.

Gunsight Ridge and **Grandads Cottage** are two other recruits who should leave their bumper performances behind them when given more of a test of stamina over hurdles. Both probably prefer better ground than they have encountered under Rules.

Kid Commando is a bright prospect for the future. Anthony Honeyball's six-year-old won by 18 lengths on his bumper debut at Fontwell and followed up with a decent second under a penalty behind Soaring Glory at Ascot before finishing fifth in a Listed contest over the same course and distance won by Israel Champ.

Switched to hurdles in the new year, he won in no more than a hack canter at Plumpton, beating subsequent winner Jack Valentine by 11 lengths, and rounded off his campaign with a thoroughly respectable third in the Grade 2 Dovecote Novices' Hurdle at Kempton in February.

Bred to stay further, Kid Commando will suit a step up in trip but he will need to settle better throughout his races, which hopefully he will learn as he matures. He looked a natural over fences in his point-to-point and it would be of little surprise if that is where we saw him next, although he could be the sort of horse who could go well in a Betfair Hurdle.

Anthony Honeyball also trains **Bleue Away** but we haven't seen her since she disappointed in a bumper at Ffos Las in November. She was a well-supported favourite that day and may have suffered a setback.

Kim Bailey's trio shaped well in their first season under Rules.

Bobhopeornohope finished third in a warm bumper at Exeter on New Year's Day but was too keen next time at Warwick and weakened back into fifth place – 49 lengths behind the winner, Bear Ghylls. Built like a chaser, he should take a step forward this season when upped in trip.

Does He Know, an English point winner, did well to finish second on his debut over two miles at Hereford where he didn't give much respect to his hurdles. He then finished within a length of the useful Listed bumper winner House Island – who later went on to finish second to Enrilo in a Grade 2 – when upped in trip to 2m 5f.

Does He Know, although lacking experience, will flourish over fences. He's a scopey sort and hurdles seem to get in his way. He remains a useful prospect.

Java Point ran well in a couple of bumpers to finish fourth to Ask A Honey Bee and then third to Getaround. Switched to hurdles, he chased home Allart at Ludlow in January and then finished fourth, keeping on well to the line, at Newbury in a race won by Chantry House.

Like many of Kim Bailey's horses, he's an attractive, big imposing chaser. Being by Stowaway out of a Monsun mare, I cannot wait to see him step up in trip to 2m 4f and beyond. He has serious potential from his mark of 119, especially on soft ground. One to follow for sure.

Dan Skelton's **River Tyne** finished tenth in the same novices' hurdle behind Chantry House having showed a little bit of promise in an all-weather bumper at Lingfield. The Geordieland mare shaped better than her finishing position suggests over hurdles, and she's one to watch when in handicaps this season.

Nicky Henderson's **Glynn** looked an exciting individual when he burst on to the scene with an impressive victory at Doncaster in January. After that he was being considered for the Festival but connections possibly felt it was too much too soon and were waiting for Aintree. He may find life tough to start with this season as he's forced out of novice company.

The more experienced **It Sure Is** will be hoping to leave some disappointing efforts behind him. He stayed on eye-catchingly into second on his debut in a decent novices' hurdle at Newbury behind Sevarano but failed to build on that in two subsequent starts and shaped like a horse who may be feeling something. If his trainer can get to the bottom of his troubles, he has the ability to bounce back.

Eclair On Line hasn't been able to get his head in front in five starts over hurdles and will probably be sent chasing this season. He looks hard to win with, but there should be a handicap opportunity for him somewhere from his mark of 104.

Similarly, **Defuture Is Bright** looks nicely poised from his rating of 101. He actually surprised me when he finished third to Flowing Cadenza on heavy ground at Ascot from a mark of 105 but I remain convinced we'll see the best of the Westerner gelding when he encounters good ground over 2m 4f or further. It wouldn't be a surprise to see him notch up a sequence of wins, he could be that well treated.

Captain Blackpearl is another who should find a winning opportunity from his mark of 114, possibly in a novices' handicap chase on a galloping track. He travelled strongly and looked the likely winner on his debut at Uttoxeter over 2m 4f but found less than expected off the bridle and was outstayed by Orrisdale. It was a similar tale of events on his next two starts, latterly when tried over 2m 1f at Carlisle in March.

He never encountered ground better than heavy and it's possible he will find improvement on a livelier surface. Also, Black Sam Bellamy's offspring can take time to fully develop.

Look Alive, also trained by Tom George, proved disappointing on his four starts under Rules. A mark of 97 could prove workable, especially if the gelding learns to settle.

Venetia Williams' **Hold That Taught** showed a good attitude to win on his hurdling debut at Lingfield (2m) but was disappointing under a penalty at Leicester when weakening tamely into fifth. He then finished 27 lengths adrift of Multellie when upped in trip to 2m 3½f at Carlisle. He should have done well for the time away from the track as he was a weak and gangly type last season. He should have enough ability to defy his mark of 119.

Emma Lavelle's **Eclair Surf** – a scopey son of Califet – was an impressive debut winner over hurdles at Exeter back in November but was no match for the competition in the Grade 1 Challow Hurdle at Newbury where he fell when out of contention. That mishap possibly left its mark as he ran disappointingly back at Exeter in March where he was soon beaten in a race won by Getaround.

I remain confident that he's a horse with a bright future and should have no problem getting back to winning ways. Soft ground and trips which bring his stamina into play are ideal.

Evander's exemplary attitude saw him win or reach the frame in all four of his completed starts last season and he will be a fun novice chaser to follow this term. He has a real zest for racing and is able to dominate a field from the front. He remains on a feasible mark of 125 over hurdles but he could easily switch to fences.

Jamie Snowden's **Exod'ela** also proved a consistent individual, placing four times before finally getting off the mark on handicap debut from a mark of 119 at Ludlow where he was fitted with a first-time tongue-tie. He was only raised 6lbs for the four-and-three-quarter-length success and looks to have plenty more to offer in that sphere. He's only small but he's a real trier and loves soft ground.

Evan Williams' lightly raced **Ballinsker** is another with an impeccable attitude, as he demonstrated when beating Evander on his debut at Ludlow. He then shaped nicely on softer ground in a Listed event at Haydock behind Thebannerkingrebel but hasn't been seen since.

With only two starts under Rules, he's an unexposed sort and should have plenty more to offer, especially on good ground where he can put his turn of foot to good use.

Fado Des Brosses was last seen staying on strongly to win a Chepstow maiden hurdle over 2m 3½f by a neck from Getaway Fred. He's a proper stayer in the making and will only improve as he matures.

Imperial Flem has not been seen since winning on his debut at Stratford back in October. He won in good style that day, but the time away from the track is a worry.

Who's The Boss performed consistently last season and I'm surprised she hasn't found a winning opportunity from a mark of 114. She has a lovely genuine attitude and is quick over her hurdles but finds herself in trouble as the race develops. Chasing over three miles on good ground may be the answer, as I'm sure there are races to be won with her.

Madera Mist was switched to fences after showing only moderate form over hurdles, but still remains a maiden after seven starts and finds herself on a low mark of 94. All bar one of her starts was on soft or heavy ground, so she may find herself more at home on better ground. She has been disappointing.

Southern Girl, Offtheshoulder, Filou Des Issards, Staithes and Mustang Alpha have already been out this season, with the former shaping with plenty of promise in behind Getaround on her hurdling debut at Perth. She should come on considerably for that and I expect her to be competitive next time.

Southern Girl

Mustang Alpha, beaten on his first two starts under Rules, shaped OK on his first outing after wind surgery over hurdles at Cartmel (2m 1f), especially having lost a shoe, but pulled up on his handicap debut (2m 7½f) at Uttoxeter when last seen. Beaten before the trip became an issue, he now has to prove his well-being.

Filou Des Issards was last of 12 on his reappearance at Fontwell in August where the good ground was probably much too quick for him. He has potential from his mark of 119 when encountering soft ground this winter.

Offtheshoulder and **Staithes** have offered little encouragement on both starts under Rules.

Over the water in Ireland, dual bumper winner **Farouk D'Alene** is a seriously useful prospect to look forward to as he embarks on his career over hurdles. The Racinger gelding is a big, raw individual and connections were mindful not to ask too much of him too soon.

When last seen he was all out to beat previous winner Fire Attack by a head and looked in desperate need of a step up in trip. He could develop into a Festival horse over 2m 4f this season.

Wide Receiver cost £410,000 after winning a point-to-point and was bought with the future very much in mind. A winner on his debut around Navan, he was last seen finishing well adrift of Appreciate It in a Grade 2 bumper at the Dublin Racing Festival at Leopardstown having chased home Eric Bloodaxe over the same course and distance in December. He looked a backward type last year and should have flourished for a summer out at grass. He could develop into a three mile novices' hurdler this term.

The third of the Gigginstown-owned Gordon Elliott-trained recruits was **Grangeclare Native**. He showed a good attitude to win on his bumper debut around Punchestown but made no impression in a Grade 2 novices' hurdle at Naas when last seen.

Geraldo was expected to make a winning bumper debut at Kilbeggan in July but was possibly unsuited by the sharp track and was beaten by his stable companion. Sent to Cork in August, he quickly left that disappointment behind him by winning impressively despite needing plenty of encouragement. Unfortunately, he suffered a suspected pelvic injury on his hurdling debut at Navan in September.

Willie Mullins' duo **Power Of Pause** and Ramillies should have more to offer this term. The former finished second in a 2m 2½f bumper at the Galway Festival in July and should be found a winning opportunity when switched to hurdles. He looked a quick horse when he won his point and may be best suited to a 2m maiden/novice hurdle on goodish ground.

Ramillies went off favourite for a competitive bumper at Leopardstown on Boxing Day but weakened into fourth inside the final furlong having travelled well throughout. With plenty of stamina in his pedigree, he may be needing a step up in trip sooner rather than later.

Henry De Bromhead has a strong team of horses to look forward to this season, and **January Jets**, formerly with Jessica Harrington, has already got off the mark for the County Waterford trainer. The Presenting gelding showed plenty of potential when mixing with some of the best novice hurdlers last term and I believe we are just scratching the surface of his ability. He could be a very high-class individual.

Telmesomethinggirl has also been making hay whilst the sun shines this summer. She seems to appreciate the better ground and could easily defy her mark of 120 when conditions are to suit.

That same comment applies to **Tune The Chello** who was last seen winning a handicap hurdle from a mark of 109 by four and a half lengths. Up to 117, she'll find life trickier, but she loves good ground and may find another opportunity before the winter comes.

Gabbys Cross hasn't troubled the judge in three starts but needs one more run to qualify for a handicap mark. He has ability but looks limited at this stage. **Bold Assassin** also needs one more run for a handicap mark.

Baptism Of Fire finished midfield in a couple of bumpers and should have more to offer when his stamina comes into play over hurdles.

Idas Boy finished second to a smart type in Tactical Move on his only start to date and will have no problem getting off the mark over hurdles when upped in trip. He's a horse with a tremendous amount of stamina and remains an exciting prospect for Noel Meade.

Paul Nolan's **Tucanae** mixed bumpers with hurdles last term, getting off the mark on the level at Limerick on Boxing Day. She's a lovely honest type, typical of Yeats mares, and will win plenty more races for her handler. 2m to 2m4f on soft ground looks ideal for her.

Runners taking three from home at the picturesque Oldcastle (Photo by Susie Cahill)

THE COURSE GLOSSARY

These courses feature throughout this book and I thought it would be a useful tool to provide a little information on their characteristics.

AGHABULLOGUE (Cork)

Left-handed course. Undulating, galloping and a proper test of stamina. Horses tend to go a good tempo around here, so you need a smooth traveller and a good jumper.

ALNWICK (Northumberland)

A left-handed course with gentle undulations. Eighteen fences are jumped over three miles and there's a long uphill pull from the fourth from home. A course which suits stayers.

BALLINDENISK (Cork)

A big right-handed course, galloping in nature. A unique course with four of the five fences on the circuit jumped on the uphill home straight – two before the line and two after the line.

BALLYARTHUR (Cork)

A big galloping left-handed track. Important to have a horse who travels and stays as the steep climb to the line takes some getting. A tough jumping test.

BALLYCAHANE (Limerick)

A largely flat left-handed course with gentle undulations in the back straight. Fifteen fences are jumped over three miles, five on each circuit with two in the home straight.

BALLYCRYSTAL (Wexford)

A new course for 2020. This left-handed track has gentle undulations with an uphill finish and fifteen fences jumped over three miles, two in the home straight on the final circuit.

BARTLEMY (Cork)

A right-handed track with long straights and a good climb for home from the second last. Inexperienced riders can kick for home too soon with the long run between the fourth and third last.

BELLHARBOUR (Clare)

One of the most picturesque tracks on the circuit. This left-handed course is a demand on stamina, despite the downhill run to the last. If the ground is soft, it can take plenty of getting.

BORRIS HOUSE (Carlow)

A big, fair, left-handed track which often produces nice ground throughout the winter months. A course where the best horse often wins.

BOULTA (Cork)

A left-handed galloping track which demands plenty of stamina. Fourteen fences are jumped in total, five on each circuit, with two on the uphill climb to the line and one past the winning post. Races can develop early but the best horses usually win. The track is also a popular schooling ground.

BADBURY RINGS (Dorset)

A rectangular, left-handed course with three sharp bends. Four fences are jumped in the home straight and there's a gradual uphill finish. Nineteen fences are jumped over three miles with two open ditches.

BROCKLESBY PARK (Midlands)

A fairly flat, left-handed track with plenty of galloping between fences.

CARRIGAROSTIG (Cork)

A new location for 2020. A one-mile, right-handed track with five fences to be jumped on each circuit – two before the winning line and one just past the post.

CASTLETOWN-GEOGHEGAN (Westmeath)

A fair, left-handed track where the horses spend much of the race on the turn. The penultimate fence in jumped at the highest point on the track and there's a good downhill run to the final fence followed by a short run-in.

CHADDESLEY CORBETT (Worcestershire)

A fairly flat, easy, left-handed track with sharp bends. Eighteen fences jumped over three miles with two fences to be jumped up the home straight on the final circuit.

CRAGMORE (Limerick)

One of the biggest tracks on the circuit. Left-handed and undulating in nature, this track takes a lot of getting, especially as the ground is usually testing. It's a major benefit for a horse to settle into a rhythm.

DOWTH HALL (Meath)

A tight left-handed track where horses are always on the turn. It's hard to make up ground from the rear of the field and there's a very sharp turn into the home straight. The final fence is met immediately after and it's a short run-in.

DROMAHANE (Cork)

This left-handed track is regarded as one of the best courses in the country and also one of the busiest. Fixtures take place on the outer track throughout the winter before switching to the inner course in the spring.

DUNGARVAN (Waterford)

Prior to 2018, this track was a figure of eight configuration, but now it is a left-handed course. Races tend to be fast and the fences come up quickly. There is over a furlong and a half run-in from the back of the last.

INCH (Cork)

A right-handed track with two long straights. It's not an easy course to come from behind and there are usually a few hard luck stories. There's a gentle pull to the line.

KILFEACLE (Tipperary)

A tough left-handed track with a good climb to the line from the third from home. The ground is often soft or heavy.

KIRKISTOWN (Down)

A fair left-handed one-mile round course. The fences are big here and offer a good jumping test for a young horse.

KNOCKANARD (Cork)

A right-handed, galloping but undulating track which requires a true stayer to get home. There's a steep descent to the second fence (from the three-mile start) and then an uphill climb to the third (also the penultimate fence).

KNOCKINROE (Tipperary)

First introduced to the calendar in 2017, this right-handed track has well-positioned fences. It's a fair track with a big, long back straight and one fence in the home straight before a short run-in.

KNOCKMULLEN HOUSE (Wexford)

A fair, right-handed track. Set over three fields, there's a long run from the third last and it can take a fair bit of stamina to get home with the final two fences taken on the climb.

LARKHILL (Wiltshire)

A wide, galloping right-handed track – the longest course in the country after Aintree. There's a steady climb over the final six furlongs which can test a horse's stamina.

LINGSTOWN (Wexford)

A big, right-handed, galloping track which usually produces drier ground due to its coastal location. Just under 10 furlongs per circuit, there is also a cross-country track here.

LISMORE (Waterford)

Another big, galloping track, almost square-like. There's a notable downhill run to the first and second fences, which are taken after the bend before turning again and climbing to fence three and four. It's not a course where you want to be in front too soon.

LISRONAGH (Tipperary)

A sharp left-handed track with a short run-in. This track suits a slick jumper and a horse who can travel. Mistakes here will quickly have you on the back foot.

LOUGHANMORE (Antrim)

A large, left-handed course but an uncomplicated course to ride. It still remains a thorough test of stamina but it's not a track biased towards hold-up horses or front runners.

LOUGHREA (Galway)

A right-handed course which can be tricky track to ride. On good ground it's a very fast, sharp track but on soft ground plenty of stamina is needed to get home. Front runners can do well here.

MAINSTOWN (Tipperary)

Left-handed course with gentle undulations. Rides like a fair track with no bias to racing handily or held up. First introduced to the point-to-point circuit in 2015.

MILBORNE ST ANDREW (Dorset)

An undulating left-handed course with an uphill climb to the last and to the line. Fences are well built and prove a proper jumping test.

MOIG SOUTH (Limerick)

This track first appeared on the calendar in 2018. A left-handed course dominated by two long straights. The final two fences are taken on the rise, with a relatively short run-in.

OLDTOWN (Dublin)

Described as one of the best pointing tracks in the country, and the nearest you can get to a standard racecourse. This right-handed track features an open ditch and three fences in the home straight. The climb to the line from the last can catch horses out.

PUNCHESTOWN (Kildare)

The pointing track is situated on the inside of the hurdles track. It's a sharp right-handed course with a good pull uphill from the third last and a long run-in. It can suit horses ridden patiently.

RATHCANNON (Limerick)

A left-handed track which takes plenty of getting on soft ground. It pays to ride a patient finish as the uphill climb to the line can catch horses out. There are two fences to be jumped in the home straight and twelve in total over three miles.

SHERIFF HUTTON (Yorkshire)

A flat left-handed course with small and very soft fences. Eighteen fences are jumped in total over three miles, two of which are open ditches.

STOWLIN (Galway)

A big, open, left-handed course with a tight turn before the penultimate fence. It helps to have a horse with a good cruising speed as there's plenty of freewheeling around here.

TALLOW (Waterford)

A flat right-handed course and one of the oldest fixtures in the calendar. Races can be run at a good pace around here and usually favours a horse with experience.

TATTERSALLS FARM (Meath)

A big, wide, right-handed, galloping track with gentle undulations and a steady pull up to the line from the third from home. Thirteen fences are jumped over three miles.

TINAHELY (Wicklow)

A galloping and undulating right-handed track with a downhill back straight and an uphill – very steep at times – home straight. It's a track which can suit an experienced horse, or a confident jumper.

TURTULLA (Tipperary)

A deceivingly sharp right-handed track with a tight bend for home and a gradual incline to the line. It pays to ride handy around here.

TYRELLA (Down)

A sharp right-handed track which dries quickly and often produces better ground than most courses. There tends to be no let-up from start to finish, so you need a horse who travels. It's very difficult to come from off the pace.

Coming down the hill at Oldtown (Photo by Susie Cahill)

Index

Star Potential Horses appear in purple

Notes

Notes

Notes